G

by
Karl Kochmann

Eighth Edition Second Printing

ISBN 0-9631669-7-2

Republished by
ClockWorks Press International, Inc.
P.O. Box 1699
Shingle Springs, California, USA
See last page for catalog information.

Copyright © 2000
by ClockWorks Press International, Inc.

TABLE of CONTENTS

CHAPTER		PAGE

- I . Foreword..1
  - . Historical location map - GUSTAV BECKER WORKS..........2
  - . Town square of Freiburg (*now Swiebodzice-Poland*).......3
  - . GUSTAV BECKER...4
  - . GUSTAV BECKER biography - *ENGLISH* -....................5
  - . UNITED FREIBURG CLOCK FACTORIES - former GUSTAV BECKER.9
- II . VORWORT - *GERMAN* - *Foreword*...........................16
  - . Firma GUSTAV BECKER................*(German)*.........17
  - . Gustav Becker Begräbnisstätte......*(German)*.........20
  - . Vereinigte Freiburger Uhrenfabriken*(German)*.........22
- III . Serial numbers on typical clock movement plate........29
  - . Trademark Index of Gustav Becker Clocks...............30
  - . Trademark Index of Gustav Becker Clocks...............31
  - . Trademark Index of Gustav Becker Clocks...............32
  - . Trademark Index of United Freiburg/Becker Works Clocks33
  - . GUSTAV BECKER ENTERPRISE - SERIAL NUMBERS.............34
  - . GUSTAV BECKER ENTERPRISE,Consolidation-Merger.........35
  - . GUSTAV BECKER, advertisement samples..................36
- IV . The 300,000 Becker Clock.............................37
  - . The 500,000 and 1,000000 Becker Clock.................38
  - . Introduction to catalogue pages 39
  - . Catalogue pages from the year 1895.................40-43
  - . Catalogue pages from the twenties..................44-59
  - . The Becker Westminster-Whittington gong-strike........60
- V . Pricelist from the twenties..........................61
  - . Pricelist from the twenties........................62-66
- VI . Excerpts from catalogue year 1933..................67-70
  - . Excerpts from catalogue (Synchron clocks).............71
  - . Excerpts from catalogue # 35 (year 1935)...........72-78
  - . Excerpts from catalogue # 42 and # 44..............79-81
  - . Excerpts from catalogue # 17.......................82-88
- VII . Selection of clocks from the authors and private archive file........ 89-107
  - A message from the author-Publisher...................109
  - Plate reference of archive material - contributors...110
  - Acknowledgements......................................111
  - Appendix GUSTAV BECKER STORY - 1992 Edition..........108
  - GUSTAV BECKER & Family year 1782 - 1885..............109
  - Plate reference - Bibliography - Literature reference.110
  - Message from the Author & Publisher..................111
  - Acknowledgments......................................112
  - Worldwide - International Book Depositories..........114
  - ANTIQUE CLOCKS PUBLISHING current PRINTINGs..........113

Photo Hennig
Hartha-Germany

Photo SCHOCK
Munich-Germany

Plate 1a
Johannes Hennig
Dresden - Germany
Year 1994

Plate 1b
Karl Kochmann
Concord-California
Year 1994

FOREWORD

The international interest in GUSTAV BECKER clocks required the need for this reprint- enlarged 8th Ed.

As horological historians, we have felt to compile this publication, to record the history of the most beautifully designed, industrially crafted and widely worldwide marketed clocks ever made. These clocks, created by GUSTAV BECKER in Germany 136 years ago, are today priceless collector's clocks all over the world.

We hope our research effort will enrich the reader in knowledge regarding the history and design of the famous timepieces created by craftsmen during the GUSTAV BECKER era.

Gustav Becker single handed founded in the year 1847 his enterprise in Freiburg (Silesia) - Germany, now after 1945 Poland. From his modest beginning, the GUSTAV BECKER enterprise interduced industrialized techniques of mass production and marketing.

The GUSTAV BECKER era did not ended with his death in the year 1885, his spirit, his creative management team carried on in the best tradition of the genious Gustav Becker. However , merger of the largest clock factories in the 1920s, economical, political , and other circumstances changed the destiny of the GUSTAV BECKER enterprise, with the end of WORLD WAR II-1945- the GUSTAV BECKER enterprise, renamed UNITED FREIBURG CLOCK FACTORIES, former GUSTAV BECKER WORKS, did not exist any more. ■

For the benefit of all readers in the German language and culture, co-author Johannes Hennig wrote the biography of GUSTAV BECKER in German. Co-author Karl Kochmann, wrote the English translation.

Concord - California
August 1995 -8th Ed.

Karl Kochmann,
Author/Private
Publisher

Johannes Hennig,
Historian,Master
Watchmaker,Author
and Lecturer

Plate 2

Historical orientation - location map of central Europe about year 1900. FREIBURG ①city- Silesia now *SWIEBODZICE-Poland*. BRAUNAU ②city- Bohemia now *BROUMOV-Czechoslovakia*. SCHRAMBERG ③ *Germany Black Forest*

Market square
Swiebodzice
(former Freiburg-
Silesia)

Plate 3

(GERMAN) Der Freiburger — The FREIBURGER

Amts-Bote   OFFICIAL GAZZETTE

Sechster Jahrgang.   Sixt year

№ 15.   No. 15

Announcement

Etablissements-Anzeige.

Hiermit gebe ich mir die Ehre, ergebenst anzuzeigen, daß ich mich hierorts Bahnhofstraße Nr. 257 a. im Hause des Hrn. Maurermeister Pasler als Uhrmacher etablirt habe. Indem ich dieses Unternehmen geneigter Beachtung empfehle und um wohlwollendes Vertrauen für dasselbe bitte, erlaube ich mir die Versicherung, daß es mein eifrigstes Bestreben sein wird, dasselbe durch streng rechtliches Wirken zu erhalten und mich dessen werth zu zeigen. Zugleich empfehle ich mein wohl assortirtes Uhren-Lager, für deren Solidität und richtigen Gang garantirt wird.

Freiburg, den 1. April 1847.

Gustav Becker.

Excerpt from the pamphlet "25 YEARS UNITED FREIBURG CLOCK FACTORIES, former GUSTAV BECKER

It is my extreme pleasure and reverend honour that I have established in the Bahnhofstrasse No. 257 in the house of the plasterer Mr. Pasler a clockmaker shop. I beg you for your patronage and confidence in my skills and I assure you it is my diligent goal to serve you honest and prudent. Also I recommand to examine the extensive selection on clocks and I guarantee good timing.

Freiburg, April 1, 1847.

GUSTAV BECKER

GUSTAV BECKER

Born May 2, 1819
    Oels, Silesia
Died September 14,
    1885

On Herrn Becker's lapel the "Golden Medal" awarded in the year 1852 during the "Silesia Trade Exhibition. "Medaille d'or" *(french)* from here on, next to the famous Becker-anchor, it was his trademark.

Plate 4

VEREINIGTE FREIBURGER UHRENFABRIKEN AKT.-GES.
INCL. VORMALS GUSTAV BECKER
FREIBURG in SCHLESIEN.

Plate 5

Graphic composition of the United Freiburg Clock Factories-Stockholder Corporation, including the former GUSTAV BECKER Works, FREIBURG / Silesia Also see historical orientation map page 2.

THE GUSTAV BECKER BIOGRAPHY *

by Johannes Hennig
© 1974

The world famous and outstanding clock factory in Silesia, former kingdom within the German-Prussian feudal regime in the city of *FREIBURG*①*(now SWIEBODZICE-Poland)* was founded by a man endowed with tremendous vigor, drive and determination combined with organizational leadership and outstanding technial talent. This man was GUSTAV BECKER.

Gustav Becker was born on May 2,1819 in Oels, Silesia. Very little is known about his early years until he was about 22 years of age. He learned the art of clockmaking in Silesia. During his travels to extend his knowledge in clockmaking which took him to german cities as well Vienna, Austria, and visiting clockmakers in Switzerland, he made eager use of every possibility to develop himself into a highly-qualified master clockmaker. In the year 1841 he was employed in Vienna in the shop of the Master Clocksmith by the name of Happacher, who was in the process of making expiremental designed and later final constructed weight driven wall regulators. There he zealously helped and participated in the development of a novel wall clock design with very outstanding features.

Two years after his return to Silesia, his home state Gustav Becker (married in the meantime) settled in 1847 as a clockmaker in Freiburg.

He turned his dream to reality to estalish a clock factory, wich he had planed in Vienna during his time in dealing with handcrafted regulator clock manufacturing in various clockshops. With great enthusiasm but very little capital, he founded it on April 1,1847 in Freiburg at the Bahnhofstrasse No.257.③ He employed in the beginning some schoolboys. During their free time he taught them filing gears and the use of a lathe. With the assistance of a few adult helpers he was able to produce a small number of regulator clocks, very similar to the Vienna design. With this modest production he was soon able to secure additional contracts with dealers.

However , the young master craftsman lacked financial assets for the procurement of machines, tools, raw material and so on. He needed a larger production location and on May 2,1850 he relocated to Ringstrasse, Number 27.④

The majority of the workers of Freiburg and the surrounding area were dependent upon cotton mills and fabric manufacturing for their livelihood. Due economic circumstances and exploitation of the working class, the poeple wer paid such poor wages that misery and financial distress were the constant companions of most families. Limited attempts of the goverment to find remedies for this hardship had so far failed. In spite of hunger and poverty, the workers were reluctant to give up their work in the mills.

Translation from German to English by Karl Kochmann
© 1974

① see page 2, plate 2.
③ see page 3, plate 3.
④ refer to page 14 plate 5a

Eventually the local goverment became aware of Gustav Becker's enterprise, and of his efforts to begin a completely new and promising business venture without the help of others. Others before him had not bee able to do this successfully.

Outsiders were very reluctant to support the founder of this clockmaking enterprise. Becker's strongest support was his own self-confidence. The precedent set by Becker's one-man enterprise was so outstanding that someone finally came to his aid, believing in Becker's potential for success. Through the efforts of the president (governor)① of Silesia, the state lawmakers intervened and assisted Becker in the establishment of a larger scale business.

In the year 1850, Becker obtained several machines for his company's use from the Royal Minister of Commerce, Herr von der Heydt. For this aid however, it was the goverment's stipulation that Becker hire about 80 boys from the poverty and famine stricken families of the cotton workers. At his own expense, he had to feed them and teach them the clockmaking craft. Besides being rather risky, this was also an immense responsibility for Becker.

Becker struggled daily with big and small setbacks. The young trainess came and went whenever they got tired of the work or for other reasons. There were not any real apprenticeship contracts available to bind them to regular work hours. It was therefore quite a challenge for Becker to build a well trained and disciplined group of skillful workers.

At the Silesian Industrial Exhibition in the year 1852, the public had the first opportunity to see and admire the BECKER regulators. Becker was awarded a state medal for his creation, and from then on used the design of that medal as his trade mark This symbol② built up more trust in his enterprise. Eventually workers from the cotton mills began to approach Becker to give them training and employment in this new innovative and promising trade of clockmaking. The ice was broken.

In the year 1854 Becker obtained some bigger contracts to manufacture office clocks for the Royal Post and Telegraph Admistration for the Kingdom of Silesia. This helped his reputation for top quality work to spread still further in the industr GUSTAV BECKER became a household word. With these successes he wa now able to secure a huge interest-free loan from the Duke of Ratibor③. Now he could finally build a casemaking shop, located in the vincinity of the railroad station, with an industrial rai road track connection. It was the beginning of a very large④ factory complex.

Becker's first simple wall regulators contained only the elementary clock movements and were meant mainly for office use. Around 1860 Becker began to manufacture more ornate cases with rich wood carving. These clocks were produced for living rooms and parlors as decorative show pieces. They were not only timepieces, but had also Westminster chimes, melodic tunes, elaborate engraved weights and pendulums. Brass, silver, gold plating was often used on the clock faces.

① Appointed by the Kingdom of Silesia
② see page 30 and 32.
③ Bohemian Nobleman and landowner under the Austrian-Hungarian Federation.
④ see page 4, plate 5.

Through his dynamic efforts, Becker overcame his greatest difficulties. His production rose dramatically. In 1875, for the 300,000 clock his company manufactured, Becker was given a signed certificate from the Emperor-Kaiser Wilhelm. Soon afterwards he was appointed to the Royal Crown Trade Commission and was honored with the crown,s gold medal.Top workmanship and reliable performance of Becker clocks earned for the Becker enterprise many further awards and certificates in exhibits around the world: London 1862,Paris 1867, Vienna 1873, Sidney 1879, Melbourne 1881, Berlin 1881, Amsterdam 1883, and Antwerp 1885.

After 1880 Becker's weight-driven regulators became practically obsolete due to competition from much cheaper produced spring-driven regulators.① These clocks were produced in very large quantities(in poorer quality) in the Black Forest of Germany②.

A bitter market rivalry startet. Becker felt himself compelled to begin manufacture of these less expensive spring-driven clocks in cheaper cases-a combination of pine and hardwood laminated with ornate decoration made from grinded wood and plaster of paris. In addition hall clocks, giant pendulum clocks modeled after a famous French type were produced.The high quality of these clocks continued to match the excellent reputation of the name "GUSTAV BECKER". Many kinds of other pleasing clock models continued to be manufactured for the export market in Europe and for overseas.

The business expanded in the meantime to 700 employees including blue collar workers.A 70 horsepower steam engine furnished the power for many specially designed machines of the clock factory.It was Becker's continuing effort to make use of the newest work methods in the tooling and machine fixture techniques. His first priority was to couple efficiency with exellence in craftsmanship.His talented workers assisted him with their own contributions to his newest ideas.Becker himself was an outstanding example for his workers, honest, and prudent. He pioneered social benefits for his workers which in those days had never been heard of before:pension plan,medical assistance, and so on.The workers felt secure and devoted their lives to the work.

While Gustav Becker was away visiting the well-know spa in Karlsbad③, on his way home on a stop over in Berchtesgaden (Germany Bavaria) on September 14. 1885 Gustav Becker passed away.
Several thousands of thankful mourners paid him their last respects at his funeral - final resting place in Freiburg - now Swibodzice, Poland - on September 17,85.
(see page 15 , plate 6 and 7)

With the Becker clock factory as a model of success, a large industry flourished. Discovering that production of regulators was more profitable business than cotton and fabric manufacturing, others followed Becker's example. A group of smaller subcontractors later established themselves in the area of Freiburg were approximately 2,000 workers were involved in the production of clocks.

①) See page 43
②) Refer to location map page 2
③) Now "Karlovy vary"Czechoslovakia

The subcontractors:	founding year:
Ender & Co.	1865
Germania	1871
Willmann Co.	1872
Sabarth	1873
Concordia	1881
Kappel & Co.	1882
Borussia	1888
Carl Boehm	1895

Most of these companies lacked qualified salesmen and managers at the outset. There developed a mighty rivalry among them. However in the year 1898 attempts were made to consider merger. Shortly before the turn of the century, on October first 1899, these small companies merged with the Gustav Becker company as a joint corporation clockfabrication in Freiburg, Silesia under the name:

"UNITED FREIBURG CLOCK FACTORIES A.G.①

formerly GUSTAV BECKER"

Until the year 1926, Becker (A.G.)② continued with a large production program of a variety of tomepieces, the 400 day clocks, show window clocks, alarm clocks, and heavy movements for grandfather clocks built to the highest perfection in the clock making art.

On or about June 1,1926, the JUNGHANS CLOCK FACTORY located in Schramberg-Black Forest ③ ,suggested a merger between JUNGHANS, the HAMBURG - AMERICAN CLOCK FACTORY, also located in Schramberg-Black Forest and the UNITED FREIBURG CLOCK FACTORIES A.G. formerly GUSTAV BECKER. The intent was to eliminate the tough competition and to exchange all possible technical knowledge. A total of 8682 employees were grouped together in this historical merger.

To indentify the products of each branch, all clocks bear their original TRADEMARK's ④. This agreement regarding the trademark rights was still in effect until the JUNGHANS CLOCK FACTORY IN SCHRAMBERG formed the:

"JUNGHANS BROTHER'S CLOCK FACTORY A.G.⑤

Dr. Buehler, member of the Junghans board of directors, represented all the interests of the Becker-Group, the Freiburg works.
World War II (ended 1945) brought an end to the GUSTAV BECKER era.

In the year 1961 the JUNGHANS-DIEHL CORPORATION, celebrated its 100th anniversary.

The GUSTAV BECKER biography would be incomplete without given credit on the following pages-excerpts-from the pamphlet:
"UNITED FREIBURG CLOCK FACTORIES A.G. formerly GUSTAV BECKER"
1899-1924

① Refer to pages 9-12
② See page
③ & ⑤ Junghans Story
   Antique Clocks Publ.1976
④ See pages 70-88

UNITED FREIBURG CLOCK FACTORIES Inc.*
Including the former GUSTAV BECKER WORKS

1899 - 1924

At the turn of the century, the stiff rivalry between the various Freiburg clockmanufactureres made itself felt. These companies also faced competition from outside factories which had begun producing *FREIBURG STYLE* pendulum clocks. So by the year 1899 the smaller companies began striving to bring together all the Freiburg clock manufacturers, in order to improve their marketing situation. It was thanks to the banking firm of E. Heiman in Breslau*(now WROCLAW-Poland)* that the leading company of Gustav Becker decided to join the merger and make the project possible, thereby forming the UNITED FREIBURG CLOCK FACTORIES. This same banking house, under the aegis of a banking syndicate, brought together the factories of Gustav Becker, including the Gustav Becker branch in Braunau-Bohemia, the Factories of A. Willman & Co., Germania, Concordia, Kappel &Co. and Boehm and established these as a corporation with capital assets of 2,700,000 Marks (Goldmarks) on June 22, 1899, as a corporation. The new corporation called itself the "Corporation for Clock Fabrication". However, in order to preserve the name of the man responsible for the Freiburg clock industry, the name was changed to*"UNITED FREIBURG CLOCK FACTORIES, Inc. including the former GUSTAV BECKER WORKS."* The first Board of Directors included the following gentlemen: E. Kuester, Chairman of the Board, Breslau; Paul Becker factory owner, Freiburg; Richard Becker, factory owner, Freiburg; Max Conrad, mill owner, Polsnitz, Wilhelm Deurer consul in Hamburg, Reinhold Jendersie, mining Inspector, retired, Breslau; Paul Landenberger, director, Schramberg Carl Marfels, publisher Berlin; and the first executive commitee: Paul Albert Becker, Max Becker and Paul Kappler.

Expected profits that has been the primary reason for forming the corporation, which included almost every company in the Freiburg area, were slow in coming. The need to reorganize the various factories into one workable unit to increase their productivity, and unify the manufactured products to one standard led to great difficulties that only circumspection and energy could overcome.

Paul Kappler, the business director left the company early 1901 to concentrate on other business opportunities and was replaced at the end of 1901 by the former general director of the Black Forest Clock industry, Josef Buehler. Taking the leading role in organizing the corporation was then the chairman of the board of directors, E. Kuester from the banking firm of E. Heiman who, in his unselfish and exceptional manner, guided and supported the company until his retirement in the year 1916. There were constant improvements in both machinery and working methods. The factories were enlarged, resulting in the operation of a totally modern leading business concern. Whereas the Gustav Becker company and the smaller businesses had concentrated on producing Viennese style pendulum clocks and travel clocks, the new corporation broadened its scope to meet practical, domestic and international artistic demands.   *Translated by Ingrid Nuernberg
© 1979

Producing marine and kitchen clocks, table, wall and free standing clocks with springs or weights, mounted in all imaginable styles of casings and incredible variety of chimes, in short, the company began building every kind of time piece for every conceivable use.

A speciality developed by the new company was the making of decor clocks with fine tuned chimes. These chimes under the names of Cathedral chimes, Harp, Regina, Eroica and Westminster chimes gained quite a reputation within the industry. The start of a new development at this phase was marked with the production of alarm clocks built after the American system in 1913 and, after World War I, with the production of pocket and other type of watches. Both of these time pieces were already being manufactured in the Black Forest. Pocket watches were also a major industry in Thuringia-Germany, however they were a new concept to the Silesian clock industry. Nevertheless, the Freiburg clock makers soon became adept at producing these watches also and manufactured them with the same precision as their other products.①

The production was divided into three factories concentrating on manufacturing all parts along with engineering-design work, brass foundry, clock face printing, glass cutting and grinding and the joiner section producing the clock casings. Only the finest and most precise machines were used in the plant. Machines of all types were at hand, from huge presses capable of exerting 250,000 kilograms of pressure to the smallest, finest machines used in the manufacturing of pocket watches. The various parts were produced under strictest quality control and were so designed as to be interchangable. This was the achieved goal in mass production.

To achieve this required a plethora of organizational work and the training of workers, before being hired, apprentices were tested by means of a phsyco-technical apparatus built by the company when hired then were taught their craft under exellent supervision in the company owned-operated trade and training school.

The same care given to the metal working section, also was given to the wood working-finishing section. Here also only the best machinery available was used. Production began with the raw log, from the saw mill, through the drying process, milling cutting, to the final assembly. The factory complex in Freiburg-Silesia and Braunau-Bohemia covered an area of 20,000 square meters and employed 2,050 workers in Freiburg, 1,300 in Braunau by the year 1899.②

But a technical organization cannot exist without a business-financial management. The distribution of orders and money had to follow one established set of guidelines. Whereas domestic revenue was handled through clock wholesale outlets sales of the international market were directed through sales representatives located all over the world. These foreign representatives proved to be very valuable, as export sales made up two-thirds of the entire production.

During the first World War, the corporation was cut off from its major export sources and could only continue production under austere conditions.

① Refer to location map page 2
② See page 15

The corporation was able to re-enter the international market after World War I with full competitivness, even though during the war foreign competition, including such new compe - titors as Italy and Japan, had virtually overtaken the field. The corporation streamlined their domestic and international market organization. A comparison in numbers will show the growth of the "UNITED FREIBURG CLOCK FACTORIES Inc."

Production Year:	Number of Workers:	Annual production of clocks based on numbers:
* 1850	15	480
* 1860	50	4,000
* 1870	300	24,000
* 1880	500	120,000
* 1890	800	105,000
1900	1,400	120,000
1913	2,300	350,000
1923	2,050	360,000

Note: Production Years marked with an * refer to the GUSTAV BECKER WORKS.

Expansion of the factories combined with inflation necessiated an increase in capital assets:

Year:	Capital:	Remarks:
1903	2,700,000 Goldmark	Decreased to: 2,250,000 Goldmark
1912	3,350,000 Goldmark	
1920	10,750,000 REICHSMARK=RM	Prefered shares in 3,000,000 RM
1921	3,000,000 RM	
1922	21,000,000 RM	Transforming 3,000,000 RM in pre-fered shares to found
	5,000,000 RM	NEW preferd shares
TOTAL CAPITAL:	33,000,000 RM	Founder shares and 5,000,000 prefered shares.

TABLE of ORGANIZATION:

Board of Directors:
Dr.Georg Heiman, commercial advisor, Breslau, chairman (1920)
Adolf Becker, bank director Breslau (1921)
Otto Schweizer, Director, Berlin (since 1902)
Dr.Hugo Sontag, Banker, Breslau (since 1921)
Ernst v.Wallenberg-Pachaly Thiergarten (since 1901)

Oskar Berl, commercial advisor, Vienna-Austria (since 1921)
Dr.W.Hoensch, director (since 1921)
V.Pohl, royal general director
Waldenburg palace, vice chairman (since 1920)
Ernst Kroitsch, Workers Repres.
Adolf Schweter, Employee's Representative
Josef Buehler, General Director (since 1901)
Max Becker, Director (Since the founding of the organization)

CONCLUSION:

Looking back over the first 25 years of the:

"UNITED FREIBURG CLOCK FACTORIES Inc.formerly GUSTAV BECKER WORKS"

it is impossble to conceive of it success without mentioning the contributions of the workers and employees of the company.

The quality of their production made the trade mark of G.B.with an anchor and a crown a symbol of excellence in the clock making industry.

Relations between managment and labor were based on mutual trust and feeling of teamwork.This is evident by the fact,on the company's silver anniversary,170 workers themselves celebrated their own 25 years with the company.Further,since the company's founding,not a single strike or lock-out was ever called.

The worker's well being was a major concern of the management.This led to the building of housing and parks for the workers.The future of the Freiburg clock industry lay in the continued good relations between management and labor and in the tradition of excellence and quality of production set by the original GUSTAV BECKER WORKS.■

A message from the publisher:

During my visit to the Black Forest in the year 1977,I had the pleasure meeting Herr GERD BENDER- Historian researcher,writer of traditional BLACK FOREST CLOCKMAKING.Herr Bender presented to me what is thought to be the only copy in existence of the original issue of:

25 YEAR ANNIVERSARY
1899- 1924
UNITED FREIBURG CLOCK FACTORIES
former GUSTAV BECKER
WORKS

This copy survived turbulent times.After World War II,Herr Bender,then in his teens,saved the copy from being used as kindling and protected it for the future.In the Year 1978 the pamphlet was printed in reduced size to compliment my publications on Historical-Industrialized Clockmaking in Europe.*

Concord,California
1983
* Out of print

KARL KOCHMANN
Author &
Private Publisher

GUSTAV BECKER'S GRAVE SITE REDISCOVERED

by Bronislaw Shicker of California
© 1983

As an acquaintance of the author of the GUSTAV BECKER STORY, I mentioned that I was planing a visit to Poland in the Fall of 1982 specifically to a town called Wroclaw (former Breslau in Silesia)①.
Mr. Kochmann, the author of several otherhistorical-technical publications on European industrial clockmaking, asked me if I could obtain some complementary information for a new revised enlarged forthcoming history of the GUSTAV BECKER clock enterprise and his family.

Mr. Karl Kochmann told me that the GUSTAV BECKER clockwork was once located in Freiburg southwest of Breslau. It was known that Gustav Becker was buried in Freiburg. Therefore Karl asked me to investigate, try to locate and possibly visit the gravesite and confirm these findings personally.

Where is Freiburg now?
According to an old German map (year 1900) compared with Polish maps, it seemed that the present town of Bolkow could be perhaps the former town of Freiburg.
Equipped with this information I left California for some "Sherlock Holmes" detective work to track down Gustav Becker's gravesite.
I narrowed my search down to an area somewhere in Poland about 100 kilometer West of Wroclaw, give or take 30 kilometers. Fortunately my project on this historical-research puzzle was not hindered much considering the circumstances at that time of political tensions and of military controls of the roadways during my visit. It might be relatively easy to find a living person. Supposedly three contacts would be enough to locate any one anywhere in the world. But to find a grave of a person who died nearly 100 years ago and was buried in one of a few dozen cemeteries in a now densely populated area was not a simple undertaken. Two World War's were fought in the area, German, Russian, Polish and other troops went back and forth over that country which suffered so much. Artillery, shells, bombing, armored tanks, pilferage, looting, anything of this kind could have destroyed the tombstone of the Becker family. Furthermore, the Becker clan moved away long time ago from the founding place of the Becker factory.

With all these uncertainties I started my search in Poland. When visiting my friend Stefan a renown Polish artist-photographer, I asked for advice and help in my search project. My friends face lightenend up the room was suddenly filled with tension, and Stefan told me that while he was recently on a landscape - photographic excursion, he noticed an interesting historical cemetery in Swiebodzice. The time and light was just right so he shot a few frames....." Please wait" he said, I have to go to my dark - room to check my negatives".....While I was waiting.....Stefan returned, he held in his hand some just developed perfect photo - graphs of the Becker family grave site ②.

cont. see page 14

① refer to location map page 2
② See page 15
③ Profile year 1989 restored
  (Foto-STEFAN-Poland)

cont.from page 13

What a spooky coincidence almost unbelievable;there is a writer in California.Here in Poland is a photographer not especially interested in clock collecting and here I am with my friend visiting Poland more than 10,000 miles away from California.
And we all together through our circumstantial independent efforts found the Gustav Becker family last resting place. Mission accomplished !
==========
The next day we visited Swiebodzice (former Freiburg). The tombstone was in style of the topwork of a grandfather clock.The gravesite was very well maintained and decorated with fresh flowers.However there were scars on the sculptured face③ profile of Gustav Becker and other parts of the stonework clearly showing the ravages this country suffered.
We all returned on a sunny day late October back to Wroclaw with the satisfaction that our historical finding and contribution to this publication would enrich the GUSTAV BECKER STORY.

One question remains still unresolved: Who decorated the gravesite with fresh flowers? Proably because the traditional memorial day for the dead on November the first was near........
Who takes care of the grave ? My friend and I went to the townhall of Swiebodzice to ask.
We were friendly received,but could not find out anything. ■

③ Profile year 1989 restored
   (Foto-STEFAN-Poland)

++++++++

Plate 5a
The historical "Ringstrasse 27" location of the GUSTAV BECKER enterprise. Refer to page 5.

Plate 5b
Detail of the clock face,also refer to page 38,plate 20.Notic< the fine detail wood carving.

Grave site of the Becker family, old cemetary near Swiebodzice (Freiburg).

Year 1982

Plate 6

Gustav Becker
Royal Trade commisioner
and Factory owner
Founder of the Freiburg
Clock Industry
born   2.May 1819
died 14.September
1885
and his wife
Louise, nee Seelig
born 14.September 1822
died 24.April 1909

The inscription read's:
(L to R)

*"Blessed are the deceased parted in the will of God.
Their work and creations will follow them"*

Revelations 14-13

Plate 7

CHAPTER II
GERMAN LANGUAGE SECTION ---- DEUTSCHE ÜBERSETZUNG
HISTORISCHER TEIL

GUSTAV BECKER STORY

✪

Herausgegeben

Karl Kochmann

© 1974

✪

1974	Ausgabe	1000
1976	Ausgabe	1000
1977	Ausgabe	1000
1983	Verbesserte Ausgabe	1000
1990	Ausgabe	1000
1992	Verbesserte Erweiterte Ausgabe	1000
1993	Ausgabe	500
1993	Nachdruck	500
1994	Ausgabe	1000
1995	Erweiterte Ausgabe	1000

1974 Copyright, Nachdruck, auch Auszugsweise nur mit schriftlicher Genehmigung.
Gedruckt in den Vereinigten Staaten von Amerika
in

ARBEITSGEMEINSCHAFT
zwischen
AMERICAN REPRINTS CO, MODESTO CAL,
95353   P.O.Box 379   U.S.A.
und
ANTIQUE CLOCKS   PUBLISHING
Concord, California   U.S.A.
FAX (510) 825 0424   A-Z Co.

Copyright Library of U.S.Congress A 770356
ISBN   093396 -33-3

FIRMA GUSTAV BECKER
© Johannes Hennig
1974

Die weltberühmte Regulator-Fabrikation in Schlesien konnte nur entstehen durch einen energischen sowie technisch und organisatorisch gut befähigten Mann wie *GUSTAV BECKER*. Am 2.Mai 1819 in Oels in Schlesien wurde Gustav Becker geboren.Dort erlernte er das Uhrmacherhandwerk.Auf seiner Wanderschaft die ihn außer in deutsche Städte auch nach der Schweiz und Wien führte,hatte er jede Gelegenheit genützt, um mit großem Lerneifer sich zu einen tüchtigen Meister heranzubilden.In Wien war er 1841 im Uhrengeschäft HAPPACHER tätig,wo gerade Gewichts-Rgulatoren berechnet und konstruiert wurden.Da half er eifrig mit und begann dort schon der Wanduhren-Konstruktion neue Wege zu bahnen.

Zwei Jahre nach Rückkehr übersiedelte Becker(inzwischen verheiratet) 1847 als Uhrmacher nach Freiburg in Schlesien. Nach weiteren zwei Jahren begann er seine Idee zu verwirklichen,die er in Wien beim Studium der handwerksmäßigen Regulatoren-Fertigung gefaßt hatte,nämlich in Schlesien eine rationelle Regulatoren-Fabrikation zu gründen.Mit großer Begeisterung und sehr wenig Mitteln gründete er die kleine Firma GUSTAV BECKER (am 1.April 1847)in zwei Stuben im Hause Bahnhofstraße 257a①und begann mit einigen Schulknaben,die er in ihrer Freizeit im Feilen und Drehen ausgebildet hatte,sowie mit ein paar Gehilfen erst einmal die handwerksmäßige Herstellung von einer kleinen Zahl Regulator-Werken (ähnlich dem Wiener Muster).Somit gelang es ihm,bald weitere Aufträge zu erhalten.Nur fehlte dem jungen,strebsamen Meister finanzielle Mittel zur Beschaffung von Maschinen,Werkzeugen und Räumlichkeit.

Hier kam ihm eine Tatsache zu Hilfe,die für die Entwicklung der Fabrik von gräßter Bedeutung war.Der größte Teil der Arbeiter von Freiburg und seiner Umgebung lebte von der Weberei. Durch wirtschaftliche Umstände hatten diese Menschen trotz großer Anstrengungen nur einso kärgliches Einkommen,daß Elend und Jammer in den Familien dieser Gegend herrschten.Alle Mühe der Regierung,dieser Krise Abhilfe zu schaffen,war bisher vergebens,da sich diese Arbeiter trotz Hunger und Armut nicht von ihrer Weberei trennen wollten.Da wurde die Regierung des Landes auf Herrn Becker aufmerksam,der allen Eifer daransetzte,in dieser Elendsgegend einen völlig neuen und aussichtsreichen Erwerbszweig aufzubauen wollen,ohne Hilfe und ohne Mittel,nur gestützt auf seine geistige Kraft.Andere vor ihm hatten das nicht fertiggebracht.

Wenn man auch dem Gründer des neuen Betriebes von allen Seiten noch keinen vollen Glauben für das Gelingen seines wagen Unternehmens schenkte,war das Vorgehen Beckers so zielbewußt,daß man bald seine zukünftigen Erfolge mit Sicherheit voraussehen mußte.

Dem Oberpräsidenten von Schlesien ist es zu verdanken, daß sich die Staatregierung für die Förderung dieser gemeinnützigen Sache einsetzte.So erhielt Becker 1850 vom Königlichen Handelsminister von der Heydt mehrere Maschinen zur Verfügung gestellt,mußte sich aber dafür 80 Knaben aus den hungernden Weberfamilien mühsam werben und auf seine Kosten in der Uhrenfabrikation ausbilden.

① Siehe Seite 2

(GERMAN)

Inzwischen fand auch die Übersiedlung im Jahre 1850 in die Räumlichkeiten Ringstrasse 27 statt.

Die Ausbildung der Lehrlinge war eine kleine Hilfe, aber auch eine große Verpflichtung. So kämpfte Becker täglich mit großen und kleinen Hindernissen, die Lehrlinge gingen wieder fort, wenn es ihnen nicht gefiel, denn Lehrverträge gab es nicht. Es war nicht leicht sich einen gut ausgebildeten Stamm von willigen Arbeitskräften zu schaffen.

Auf der Schlesischen Industrie-Aussstellung(1852) waren erstmalig Beckers Regulatoren zu bewundern. Die dort erhaltene Staatsmedaille förderte das allgemeine Vertrauen zu diesem Unternehmen. Langsam kamen die ehemaligen Weber selbst und suchten hier Anstellung und sicheres Brot zu finden, der Bann war gebrochen. 1854 erhielt Becker größere Aufträge von der königlichen Post-und Telegraphenbüros für Dienstuhren. Das verhalf ihm zu einer schnellen Verbreitung seines Rufes für Qualitätsarbeit. Der Name Becker wurde ein Begriff. Für sein Streben und seine Erfolge erhielt er 1856 durch den Herzog von Ratibor eine größere zinsfreie Kapitalsanleihe. Nun konnte er endlich eine eigene Gehäuse-Tischlerei in der Nähe des Bahnhofes aufbauen, den Grundstock zu der späteren großen Fabrik.

Die ersten Regulator-Uhren besaßen nur Gehwerk und waren für Büros gedacht. Um 1860 wurden nun auch reicher verzierte Gehäuse für Wohnräume gefertigt, die ausser Geh-auch Schlagwerke enthielten. Durch Beckers zähen Willen waren nun auch die größten Schwierigkeiten beseitigt und die Fabrikationszahlen stiegen gewaltig an. Für die 100.000 Uhr erhielt 1875 der verdiente Schöpfer dieses Betriebes ein von Sr. Majestät des Kaisers Wilhelm unterzeichnetes Anerkennungsschreiben und wurde bald danach zum Kgl. Kommisionsrat ernannt und erhielt den Kronenorden.

Die vorbildliche Konstruktion und saubere Ausführung seiner Uhren brachten ihm auf vielen Austellungen Anerkennung und hohe Auszeichnungen ein (London 1862, Paris 1867, Philadelphia 1872, Wien 1873, Sidney 1879, Melbourne 1881, Berlin 1881, Amsterdam 1883, und Antwerpen 1885.

Nach 1880 wurde der bei Becker gefertigte Gewichtszug-Regulator immer mehr durch den viel billigeren Federzug-Regulator verdrängt, der jetzt in großen Mengen mit geringer Qualität des Werkes im Schwarzwald produziert wurde. Es begann ein harter Konkurrenzkampf, und auch in Schlesien mussten billigere Federzug-Werke in noch billigeren und reicher verzierten Gehäusen gefertigt werden. Weiter aufgenommen wurde die Fabrikation
   von Reise-Pendelweckern nach französischen Muster. Die hohe Qualität der Erzeugnisse und damit der gute Ruf des Namens "BECKER" wurden jedoch immer gewahrt.

Der Betrieb war inzwischen auf 700 Beschäftigte angewachsen. Eine Dampfmaschine mit 70 PS trieb die vielen Maschinen des Werkes an. Auch war es laufend Bekers Bestreben, stets die neuesten Arbeitsmethoden-vor allem rationelle Arbeitsteilung - anzuwenden. Ein Stamm talentierter Mitarbeiter umgab ihn und half ihm bei der Verwirklichung all seiner neuen Ideen. Ihnen war er stets ein gutes Vorbild. Auch für das soziale Wohl seiner Arbeiter tat er alles was möglich war.

(GERMAN)

Auf der Heimreise von einer Genesungskur in Karlsbad im Jahre 1885, bei einen Zwischenaufenthalt in Bayern im Kurort Berchtesgaden, verschied Gustav Becker am 14.September 1885.
Viele Tausende dankbarer Menschen gaben ihm am 17.Sept. 1885 in Freiburg (nun Swibodcize - Poland) das letzte Geleit zu seiner Ruhestätte.
(siehe Seite 15 , Abbildung 6 und 7)

♦

Seinem großen Vorbild nacheifernd waren in den letzten Jahren in der dortigen Gegend viele kleinere Unternehmungen gegründet worden,als man gemerkt hatte,daß die Fertigung von Regulatoren doch ein einträglicheres Geschäft darstellt als die Weberei.So ist es auch indirekt als das Werk Beckers anzusehen,daß bald in der ganzen Gegend von Freiburg cirka 2000 Arbeiter in der Hausuhren-Fabrikation tätig waren.Es waren dies die Firmen Ender &Co.(1865),Germania(1871),Willmann& Co. (1872),Babarth(1873),Concordia(1881),Kappel&Co.(1882)Borussia (1888),und Carl Boehm(1895).Bei all diesen Betrieben fehlten meist tüchtige Kaufleute und Organisatoren und ein heftiger Konkurrenzkampf untereinander setzte ein.Deshalb entfalteten sich im Jahre 1898 Bestrebungen zu einer geschäftlichen Vereinigung.

◇

Kurz vor der Jahrhundertwende-am 1.10.1899-schlossen sich dann all die kleinen Betriebe mit der Firma Gustav Becker zusammen als eine Aktiengesellschaft für Uhrenfabrikation in Freiburg in Schlesien unter dem Namen:"*VEREINIGTE FREIBURGER UHRENFABRIKEN AKTIENGESELLSCHAFT vormals GUSTAV BECKER*".Es war die über Deutschlands Grenzen hinaus angesehenste Fabrik mit der Herstellung von Gewichts-und Federzug-Regulatoren sowie Freischwinger-,Marine-Sekunden,Jahres-,Haus-und Schaufensteruhren mit massiven Werken in höchster Vollendung.

Bis 1926 arbeitete diese Aktiengesellschaft mit einem breiten Fertigungsprogramm.Am 1.7.1926 wurde auf Anregung der Firma JUNGHANS A.G.in Schramberg(Schwarzwald)eine Interessengemeinschaft zwischen den beiden Schwarzwälder Uhrenfabriken "JUNGHANS A.G.)und der "HAMBURG-AMERIKANISCHE UHRENFABRIK"in Schramberg-Schwarzwald sowie "VEREINIGTE FREIBURGER UHREN - FABRIKEN vorm.GUSTAV BECKER" ins Leben gerufen,um einen gegenseitigen Konkurrenzkampf auszuschalten und den Erfahrungsaustausch untereinander zu fördern.Die Kennzeichnung mit den Warenmarken der in einzelnen Betrieben hergestellten Uhren wurde beibehalten.Diese Kennzeichnung blieb sogar noch erhalten, als am 1.7.1930 die Firma JUNGHANS A.G.sich mit den beiden anderen Großbetrieben zusammenschloss unter dem Namen: "UHRENFABRIKEN GEBRÜDER JUNGHANS A.G."

Als Vorstandsmitglied in diesem Großbetrieb,mit über 9000 beschäftigten Betriebsangehörigen,vertrat Herr Dr.Buehler die Interessen des Werkteiles Freiburg-Schlesien.

Der 2.Weltkrieg brachte das Ende der Firma GUSTAV BECKER.■

◇

(GERMAN)

GUSTAV BECKER BEGRÄBNISSTÄTTE WIEDER ENTDECKT.*

© 1982 Bronislaw Shicker
of California

In einen Gespräch mit meinem Bekannten Herrn Karl Kochmann der im selben Bezirk wie ich in Kalifornien lebt,erwähnte ich,daß ich im Herbst 1982 den Plan hatte nach Polen zu reisen und daß ich mich hauptsächlich in der Stadt Wroclaw (früher Breslau in Schlesien) aufhalten wollte.

Herr Kochmann,ein Uhrenliebhaber und Sammler,der bereits mehrere Schriften über Europäische Uhrenbauer und ihre Fabrikationsstätten geschrieben hat,bat mich ob ich eventuell versuchen könnte auch nach Freiburg in Schlesien zu reisen,um dort einige Daten über Gustav Becker,seine Familiengeschichte und Uhrenfabrik ausfindig zu machen,da er diese Daten für eine neue erweiterte Auflage seines Gustav Becker Buches brauchte.

Es war auf Grund der vorausgegangenen Nachforschungen mit großer Sicherheit festgestellt worden,daß Gustav Becker in Freiburg beerdigt worden war.Der Ort und die genaue Lage des Grabes war nach wie vor unbekannt,doch waren wir beide der Ansicht daß ein persönlicher Besuch nach Freiburg und Umgebung vieleicht von Erfolg sein könnte.

Wo liegt Freiburg nun? Wir verglichen alte deutsche Landkarten mit neuen polnischen Landkarten und kamen zu der Überzeugung daß die Stadt Bolkow vieleicht die ehemalige deutsche Stadt Freiburg sein könnte.Mit diesen mageren Informationen und einer Flugkarte über die halbe Welt von Kalifornien nach Polen ausgestattet,begann ich meine Sherlock Holmes Aufgabe die Begräbnisstätte Gustav Becker's ausfindig zu machen.

Es ist im Allgemeinen nicht schwer eine noch lebende Person zu finden wenn man zwei Anhaltspunkte hat,Name und Ort.Aber in diesem Falle handelte es sich um eine Person,die vor fast 100 Jahren in einem der vielen Friedhöfen dort beerdigt worden war, als das Land noch deutsch war.Nun ist es polnisch und fast nur Polen leben dort,neu angesiedelt von der Regierung nachdem die Deutschen im Jahre 1945 das Land verlassen mußten.Diese Menschen konnten mir sicherlich nicht behilflich sein,da sie wahrscheinli nie etwas von Gustav Becker gehört hatten.Auch ist es bekannt,da die Friedshofsverwaltungen im allgemeinen in dicht besiedelten Gegenden,die Grabstätten nach 30 Jahren auflösen.100 Jahre ist e lange Zeit,2 Weltkriege hatten stattgefunden,russische,polnische und andere Truppeneinheiten waren durch das Land gezogen,Bomben und Granaten hatten es zerstört,bestand das Grab wirklich noch? Je näher ich dem Reiseziel kam umso hoffnungsloser schien mir di ganze Sache zu sein.

In Wroclaw angekommen,besuchte ich sofort meinen Freund Stefa einen bekannten Künstler-Photograph,ich bat ihn mir bei meiner Su behilflich zu sein.Noch während ich sprach hellte sich sein Gesicht auf und er lächelte geheimnissvoll.Er erzählte mir,daß e vor einiger Zeit,auf der Suche nach historischen Motiven in der schlesischen Landschaft,einen alten Friedhof in Swiebodzice entdeckt hat und da die Tageszeit und Lichtverhältnisse gut waren hat er ein paar Gräber photographiert."Warte hier ich gehe in meine Dunkelkammer und werde ein paar Aufnahmen entwickeln". So wartete ich,endlich kam Stefan zurück.Er hielt in seinen Händen die eben entwickelten perfekten Abzüge der Becker Gruft i Freiberg.

* Übersetzung englisch-deutsch
© 1982 Karl Kochmann

Welch ein Zufall, unglaublich und fast unwahrscheinlich.
Da ist ein Author in Amerika, hier ein polnischer Photograph, nicht besonders interessiert an der Uhrentechnik und ich ein Freund von beiden, und wir alle drei haben unabhängig von einander durch zufallsreiche Umstände die Grabstätte Gustav Beckeräs und seiner Familie wieder entdeckt. Ein paar Tage später reisten wir zuammen nach Swiebodzice (Freiburg) und besuchten die Grabstätte.

Sie war in gutem Zustand. Die Mitte des Grabsteines hat die Form des Oberteiles einer Standuhr der damaligen Zeit. Die Witterungseinflüsse und wahrscheinlich Kriegseinwirkungen hatten das Marmorprofil*von Gustav Becker ganz wenig beschädigt. Das Grab machte einen gepflegten Eindruck und es war sogar mit frischen Blumen dekoriert.**
** Wir hätten gerne gewusst wer der Pfleger war, aber alle unsere Erkundigungen hatten in dieser Beziehung keinen Erfolg.

Doch hatte ich ein gutes Gefühl, meine Mission war erfolgreich abgeschlossen.

Anmerkung des Publisher :
* Der Friedhof steht unter Kulturschutz von der Polnischen Regierung. Das Marmorprofil ist im Jahre 1989 restauriert worden (Bronislaw Shicker)
**
Durch eine Leserzuschrift an Antique Clocks Publishing , wurde mitgeteilt, daß Nachkommen der Becker Familie in der Schweiz lebend, die Grabstätte ihrer Vorfahren pflegen.

Die Biographie über GUSTAV BECKER und sein Lebenswerk wäre nicht vollständig ohne die gebührende Erwähnung Freiburger Uhrenindustrie, welche in der Festschrift:
" 25 JAHRE VEREINIGTE FREIBURGER UHRENFABRIKEN A.G.
incl. vormals GUSTAV BECKER"
im Jahre 1924 veröffentlicht wurde.
Auf den nachfolgenden Seiten 22 bis 28 ist in Faksimilwiedergabe der Satzspiegel - verkleinert - von der Größe des Orginals 23 x 30 centimeter dann dem Format des vorliegenden Buches angepaßt.

Platte 7A

Stempelmarke Zum Haupt...... wir die Beibringung des Wertstempel
zum....... ist eine Gebuehr von M 1,50...........

VERTRAGSABKOMMEN

Zu den mit den Uhrenfabrikanten G.B.in Freiburg/Schlesien wegen Lieferung von Amtszimmeruhren-Regulatoren fuer die Post und Telegraphenanstalten unter dem 21/23 November 1863 abgeschlossenen Vertrag.

Im Auftrag des Kaiserlichen General Postamtes und mit Vorbehalt in Genehmigung desselben ist heute zwischen Herrn der Kaiserlichen Postamt in Freiburg/Schlesien.......von der zu Westen und dem Uhrenfabrikanten Herrn Gustav Becker in Freiburg/Schlesien nachstehender Nachtrag zu den Vertrage dem 21/23......Uhr geschlossen worden.
Par. 1
Herr G.Becker erklaert sich bereit die im Vertrag vom...November 1863 zu liefernden Amtszimmeruhren........von jetzt ab.....Mark...
.....60 Pfennig fuer das Stueck zu ermaessigen.i
Par.2
Alle ueberigen Vereinbarungen/Bestimmungen im Vertrag vom 21/23 November 1863 bleiben in Kraft.
Par.3
Die gesetzlichen Stempelkosten fuer das Nachtrags Abkommen trägt der Unternehmer.
Gegenwärtiger Nachtrag ist zweifach gleichlautend ausgefertigt und von beiden......unter zuziehung zweier Zeugen unterschrieben worden.
Freiburg Schlesien 25.April 1871
Unterschrift:
(Stempel)
GUSTAV BECKER

Königl.Deutsches   Von zur Westen   A.Friedrich Bruckner
Postamt   Postdirektor   ..... Inspektor
Freiburg   SIEGEL   Unterschrift Zeugen
                                      ....

Publisher Anmerkung: ......Punktierte Satzunterbrechung das
                     Wort in der Faksimilie unlesserlich.

21

(GERMAN)

III.
Vereinigte Freiburger Uhrenfabriken A. G.
incl. vormals Gustav Becker
1899–1924

Um die Wende des vorigen Jahrhunderts hatte sich der Wettbewerb der Freiburger Uhrenfabriken untereinander recht drückend fühlbar gemacht. Auch auswärtige Fabriken hatten die Herstellung von Freiburger Gewichtpendeluhren aufgenommen, sodaß im Jahre 1898 die kleineren Uhrenfabriken eine Besserung ihrer Lage durch einen alle Freiburger Uhrenfabriken umfassenden Zusammenschluß anstrebten. Es war das Verdienst des Bankhauses E. Heimann in Breslau, die führende Firma Gustav Becker ebenfalls für das Projekt zu gewinnen und die Vereinigung der Freiburger Uhrenfabriken herbeizuführen. Das genannte Bankhaus erwarb im Auftrage eines Banken-Konsortiums die Uhrenfabriken von Gustav Becker nebst deren Zweigniederlassung Braunau i. Böhm., ferner die Fabriken A. Willmann & Co., Germania, Concordia, Kappel & Co. und C. Böhm und brachte diese Fabriken in eine am 22. Juni 1899 mit einem Kapital von Mk. 2 700 000 neugegründete Aktiengesellschaft ein. Die neue Gesellschaft firmierte zuerst »Aktien=Gesellschaft für Uhrenfabrikation«. Um aber den Namen des Begründers der Freiburger Uhrenindustrie der Nachwelt zu erhalten, wurde die Firma in »Vereinigte Freiburger Uhrenfabriken Aktien=Gesellschaft incl. vorm. Gustav Becker« umgeändert. Den ersten Aufsichtsrat der Gesellschaft bildeten die Herren: E. Küster, Vorsitzender, Breslau, Paul Becker, Fabrikbesitzer, Freiburg, Richard Becker, Fabrikbesitzer, Freiburg, Max Conrad, Mühlenbesitzer, Polsnitz, Wilhelm

Salonuhr
Saloon clock

Plate 8

GENERAL NOTE:
Pages 22 to 28 are selected excerpts from the pamphlet:
"25 YEARS UNITED FREIBURG CLOCK FACTORIES, former GUSTAV BECKER." Also refer to the note on page 12.

(GERMAN)

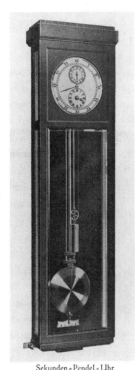

Sekunden‑Pendel‑Uhr
Watchmaker regulator

Deurer, Konsul, Hamburg, Reinhold Jendersie, Berginspektor a. D., Breslau, Paul Landenberger, Direktor, Schramberg, Carl Marfels, Zeitungs‑Verleger, Berlin, und den ersten Vorstand die Herren: Paul Albert Becker, Max Becker und Paul Kappler.

Die durch den Zusammenschluß erhofften großen Erfolge blieben für die neue Gesellschaft, welche jetzt die Freiburger Uhrenindustrie fast restlos umfaßte, zunächst aus. Die Notwendigkeit, die verschiedenen Fabriken in Bezug auf Betriebs‑ und Absatzorganisation auf eine einheitliche Grundlage zu stellen, ihre Leistungsfähigkeit zu erhöhen und die Erzeugnisse zu normen, brachte vielerlei Schwierigkeiten mit sich, die nur durch größte Umsicht und Tatkraft der Leitung überwunden werden konnten.

Schon im Jahre 1901 schied der kaufmännische Direktor, Paul Kappler, aus den Diensten der Gesellschaft, um sich an anderweitigen Unternehmungen zu beteiligen, und an seine Stelle trat Ende 1901 der aus der Schwarzwälder Uhrenindustrie hervorgegangene jetzige Generaldirektor Josef Bühler.

Hervorragenden Anteil an der Organisation des Unternehmens hatte der damalige erste Vorsitzende des Aufsichtsrates E. Küster vom Bankhause E. Heimann, der in vorbildlicher und selbstloser Weise bis zu seiner Amtsniederlegung im Jahre 1916 sein reiches Wissen der Gesellschaft zur Verfügung stellte und den Vorstand mit Rat und Tat unterstützte. Es wurden sowohl die maschinellen Einrichtungen wie auch die Arbeitsmethoden andauernd verbessert, die Betriebe erweitert, sodaß im Laufe der Jahre ein moderner Großbetrieb entstand. Während die Firma Gustav Becker und ihre kleineren Konkurrenten das Hauptgewicht auf die Herstellung von Wiener Pendeluhren und Reiseweckern legte, ging die neue Gesellschaft immer mehr dazu über, ihre Erzeugnisse den vielfältigen, praktischen Bedürfnissen sowie der Geschmacksrichtung der in‑ und ausländischen Märkte sorgfältig anzupassen und das Fabrikationsprogramm dementsprechend

Plate 9

(GERMAN)

von Jahr zu Jahr zu vergrößern, sodaß nach und nach Jahres=, Marine= und Küchenuhren, Tisch=, Wand= und Standuhren mit Feder= und Gewichtzug in allen Holz= und Stilarten und mit den kompliziertesten Gong=Schlag= werken, ferner feinmechanische Lauf= und Zählwerke aller Art für die verschiedensten Gebrauchs= zwecke hergestellt wurden.

Ein von der neuen Gesell= schaft mit großem Erfolg ge= pflegtes Spezialgebiet ist die Herstellung von Zimmeruhren mit feingearbeiteten Gong= Schlagwerken, die sich unter der Bezeichnung Domgong, Harfen=, Regina=, Eroica=, Westminster = Gong etc. in der Fachwelt einen besonderen Namen gemacht haben.

Den Beginn einer neuen Entwicklungs = Periode stellt die Aufnahme der Wecker= Fabrikation nach amerika= nischem System im Jahre 1913 und ferner die Aufnahme der Taschenuhren = Fabrikation nach dem Kriege dar. Beide Fabrikationsarten waren bereits im Schwarz= wald, die Taschenuhrenfabrikation auch in Thüringen heimisch, bedeuteten aber für die schlesische Uhrenindustrie technisches Neu= land. Inzwischen ist es gelungen, auch diese neuen Fabrikations = Abteilungen auf eine hohe Stufe der Entwicklung zu bringen,

Präzisions = Uhrwerk
Precision movement

sodaß ihre Erzeugnisse den guten Ruf der Freiburger Uhren mehren helfen.

Die Fabrikation gliedert sich in drei Metall= bearbeitungsbetriebe, in denen die Uhrwerke hergestellt werden mit ihren Nebenbetrieben wie: Maschinenfabrik, Gürtlerei, Metalldrük= kerei, Gelbgiesserei, Ziffer= blattdruckerei, Glasschleiferei und einen Holzbearbeitungs= betrieb mit Sägewerk und zahlreichen Abteilungen, in denen die Uhrgehäuse her= gestellt werden. Die Metalle werden vorwiegend mittels Werkzeug = Automaten von höchster Präzision und Lei= stungsfähigkeit bearbeitet. Es gibt kaum eine Gattung von Metallbearbeitungs=Maschi= nen, die in den Betrieben nicht vorhanden wäre, von schwe= ren Pressen von 250 000 kg Druckleistung angefangen bis zu den feinsten, meist im eigenen Betriebe hergestellten Maschinchen in der Taschen= uhrenfabrikation, deren minu= tiöse Präzisionsarbeit man nur mit dem Vergrößerungsglase erkennen kann und bei denen sich Genauigkeitsgrenzen von 0.02 mm ergeben. Die Herstellung der einzelnen Teile erfolgt unter weitestgehender Kontrolle und so schablonenmäßig, daß sie austauschbar sind. Es ist dies ein für jede Massenfabrikation anzustrebendes Höchst=

Plate 10

(GERMAN)

Weckerwerk
Alarm Clock movement

ziel. Bis es erreicht war, mußte eine Fülle von Organisationsarbeit geleistet und ein Stamm tüchtiger Facharbeiter herangebildet werden.

Der Ausbildung des Facharbeiter=Ersatzes wird große Sorgfalt gewidmet. Die Lehrlinge werden vor Einstellung mittels im eigenen Betriebe hergestellter psychotechnischer Ap= parate einer Eignungsprüfung unterzogen und ihre Fachausbildung durch eine eigene, unter vorzüglicher Leitung stehende Werkschule unterstützt.

Ebenso wie die Metalle werden auch im Holzbearbeitungsbetriebe die Hölzer ma= schinell bearbeitet, und auch hier ist rationelle Herstellung und Arbeitsteilung Grundsatz. Der Fabrikationsgang fängt beim rohen Baum= stamm an, wie er im Walde gefällt wird und läuft dann lückenlos über das Sägewerk, die Trocknungsanlagen, die Maschinensäle, die Polier= und Zusammenbau=Werkstätten. Die Betriebe in Freiburg und Braunau be= decken einen bebauten Flächenraum von 20000 qm, benötigen etwa 1000 PS an Licht und Kraft und beschäftigen rund 2050 Arbeiter und Angestellte gegen 1300 im Jahre 1899.

Hand in Hand mit der technischen Orga= nisation ging die kaufmännische. Auch der Vertrieb mußte auf eine einheitliche Grund= lage gestellt werden. Während im Inland der Absatz mittels der Großhändler des Faches an die Uhrmacher erfolgt, wurden zur Pflege des Exportgeschäftes an den wichtigsten Handelsplätzen aller Erdteile Vertretungen mit Musterlagern errichtet. Dieser weit ver= zweigten Auslandsorganisation entsprechend ist auch der Export ein sehr bedeutender; er beträgt etwa zwei Drittel der gesamten Produktion.

Taschenuhrwerk
Pocket watch

Während des Weltkrieges war die Gesell= schaft von ihren wichtigsten ausländischen Absatzgebieten abgeschnitten und konnte die Uhrenfabrikation nur in bescheidenem Um= fange aufrecht erhalten. Die Produktionskraft

Plate 11

(GERMAN)

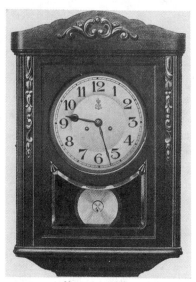

Herrenzimmer-Uhr
Gentlemen - Study clock

Einige vergleichende Zahlen mögen den geschilderten Entwicklungsgang der Gesellschaft ergänzen:

Produktionsjahr	Arbeiterzahl	Jahresproduktion an Uhren u. Uhrwerken nach Stückzahl
*1850	15	480
*1860	50	4 000
*1870	300	24 000
*1880	500	120 000
*1890	800	105 000
1900	1 400	120 000
1913	2 300	350 000
1923	2 050	360 000

Die mit * versehenen Produktionsjahre betreffen die Firma Gustav Becker.

mußte in den Dienst der Landesverteidigung gestellt werden. Zahlreiche Beamte und Arbeiter mußten dem Rufe zur Verteidigung des Vaterlandes folgen. Von ihnen sind 53 auf dem Felde der Ehre gefallen; eine Gedenktafel im Verwaltungsgebäude der Gesellschaft hält die Erinnerung an diese Tapferen wach. Daß es nach Beendigung der Feindseligkeiten gelang, die geschäftlichen Beziehungen im In- und Auslande wieder in vollem Umfange aufzunehmen, obgleich in den Kriegsjahren ausländische Konkurrenz, auch neu entstandene, z. B. in Japan und Italien, ihr den Absatz allenthalben streitig zu machen suchte, zeugt von der starken Stellung, die sich die Freiburger Uhren im Laufe der Jahre auf dem Weltmarkt geschaffen haben.

Ausbau und Erweiterung der Betriebe sowie die Geldentwertung der letzten Jahre machten mehrfache Kapitalserhöhungen notwendig. Das im Jahre 1903 von ursprünglich Mk. 2 700 000 auf Mk. 2 250 000 herabgesetzte Kapital wurde erhöht:
im Jahre 1912 um M. 1 000 000
im Jahre 1920 um M. 10 750 000
im Jahre 1921 um M. 3 000 000 Vorzugsaktien
im Jahre 1922 um M. 21 000 000 unter Umwandlung von M. 3 000 000 Vorzugsaktien in Stammaktien und unter Schaffung von M. 5 000 000 neuer Vorzugsaktien,
sodaß das Gesamtkapital aus M. 33 000 000 Stammaktien und M. 5 000 000 Vorzugsaktien besteht.

Der Verwaltung gehören zur Zeit folgende Herren an:

Plate 12

(GERMAN)

Aufsichtsrat:

Dr. jur. Georg Heimann, Kommerzienrat, Breslau, Vorsitzender ⟨seit 1901⟩,
v. Pohl, Fürstl. Pleß'scher Generaldirektor, Schloß Waldenburg, stellvertretender Vor= sitzender ⟨seit 1920⟩,
Adolf Becker, Bankdirekt., Breslau ⟨seit 1921⟩,
Oskar Berl, Kommerzialrat, Wien ⟨seit 1921⟩,
Dr. W. Hönsch, Reg.Baumeister u. Direktor, Breslau ⟨seit 1920⟩,
Otto Schweitzer, Direktor, Berlin ⟨seit 1902⟩,
Dr. Hugo Sontag, Bankier, Breslau ⟨seit 1921⟩,
Ernst von Wallenberg=Pachaly, Ritter= gutsbesitzer, Thiergarten, Kreis Wohlau ⟨seit 1901⟩,
Adolf Schweter, als Vertreter der Ange= stellten,
Ernst Kroitzsch, als Vertreter der Arbeiter.

Vorstand:

Generaldirektor Josef Bühler ⟨seit 1901⟩, Direktor Max Becker ⟨seit Gründung der Gesellschaft⟩.

Beim Rückblick über das in 25jähriger be= harrlicher Arbeit Geschaffene ist es Ehren= pflicht, derjenigen dankbar zu gedenken, die in erster Linie berufen waren, zum Erfolge beizutragen, nämlich der Angestellten und Arbeiter des Unternehmens. Die hohe Qua= litätsarbeit, die den Erzeugnissen mit der weltbekannten Schutzmarke G.B. mit Anker und Krone nachgerühmt wird, hat zu den Erfolgen der Vergangenheit geführt, und sie wird auch für die Zukunft der Freiburger Uhren=Industrie entscheidend sein. Sie setzt einen Stamm tüchtiger Facharbeiter unter ziel= bewußter technischer Leitung voraus. Das Ver=

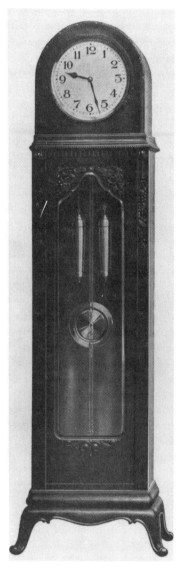

Salonuhr

Saloon clock

Plate 13

(GERMAN)

hältnis zwischen Firma und Werksangehörigen ist von jeher von dem für eine gedeihliche Zusammenarbeit unerläßlichen gegenseitigen Vertrauen getragen worden, wovon die Tatsachen, daß 170 Werksangehörige zugleich mit dem Jubiläum der Gesellschaft ihr eigenes Dienstjubiläum feiern, und daß es seit Bestehen der Gesellschaft weder eines Streiks noch einer Aussperrung bedurfte, um Meinungsverschiedenheiten auszutragen, beredtes Zeugnis ablegen. Das Wohl der Werksangehörigen bildet die stete Sorge der Leitung, so wurde der Wohnungsnot durch Errichtung von Werkwohnungen und Gartenanlagen gesteuert. In dem Weiterbestand des guten Verhältnisses zwischen Unternehmen und Werksangehörigen und in der traditionellen Beckerschen Qualitätsarbeit liegt die beste Aussicht für die Zukunft der Freiburger Uhrenindustrie und der in ihr Beschäftigten.∎

Kaminuhr mit Westminsterspiel

```
Mantle clock with
Westminster chimes
```

19

Plate 14

CHAPTER III
Serial number on typical BECKER CLOCK PLATE.

Plate 15
Typical GUSTAV BECKER LOGO on CLOCK PLATE.
Additional reference see page 31-35.

TRADEMARK OR TRADENAME MARQUE DE FABRIQUE - NOMS WARENZEICHEN - WORTMARKE	NAMES AND ADDRESSES NOMS ET ADDRESSES NAMEN UND ADDRESSEN	REMARKS OBSERV'TN BEMERKUNG
B E C K E R GUSTAV **Gustav Becker in Freiburg in Schlesien.**  	BECKER, Gustav operated : GUSTAV BECKER- UHRENFABRIK (Clock Factory) Freiburg / Schlesien now: "Poeple Republic Poland" Germany Gustav Becker ✲ 02.05.1819 , + 17.09.1885. the founder of the giant GUSTAV BECKER WORKS, by education -clockmaker of the Viennese School, announced April 01.1847, to open his clock shop in Freiburg / Silesia. It was a modest beginning, struggle,set = backs until the Prussian State provided funds to relieve the chronic unemployement in the very Freiburg district. Year after year the Gustav Becker enterprise came in the foucus of the world clock market. During the Silesian Trade exhibition , year 1854,the BECKER clocks received numerous awards, later known as : Medaille d' or (French) embossed on the back of of clock movements and registered under the Trade Symbol protection. See page 310 for reference. The Gustav Becker enterprise employed during their peack product. over 1000 employees. The Becker Clock Factory, continued under various merger/reorganizations until the year 1926, see page 35 GUSTAV BECKER Freiburg - Silesia Germany (now Poland) Trademark registered 3.July 1875. Wall,hall,regulator, GUSTAV BECKER Freiburg- Silesia Germany - (now Poland) Trademark since December 1883. GUSTAV BECKER Freiburg-Silesia Germany (Now Poland) 028/4 Trademark on backplate: Two Gustav Becker seals Registered 10.Nov.1887. And later reregistered date..........?	

NOTE: Additional chronological data
see page 109

REMARKS OBSERV'TN BEMERKUNG	NAMES AND ADDRESS NOMS ET ADDRESSE NAMEN UND ADDRESSE	TRADEMARK OR TRADENAME MARQUE DE FABRIQUE - NOMS WARENZEICHEN - WORTMARKE
	GUSTAV BECKER Freiburg - Silesia Germany (now Poland) 034/4 Trademark: German Eagle with GUSTAV BECKER and crown. Registered 01.March 1900 and October 1900.	GUSTAV BECKER
	Germany 090/16 Trademark symbol of the Gustav Becker enterprize, after merger and reorganization 14.05.1901, under: VEREINIGTE FREIBURGER UHRENFABRIKEN, former Gustav Becker Works.	
	Germany 091/16 Trademark, VEREINIGTE UHRENFABR FREIBURG, Gustav Becker Works. (United Freiburg Clock Factories) former Gustav Becker Works) Registered 16.07.1903.	
	Germany 092/16 Embossement on clock backplate: GUSTAV BECKER, E = Pendulumn lenght P35 (cm) centimeter F = Vibration SCH 118/ minute G = Silesia (englisch) Schlesien	
	Germany (now Poland) 032/4 Typical embossement on clock backplate: A Pendulumn lenght B German Patent No. C Registration No. D Serial Number	
	GUSTAV BECKER Braunau-Bohemia * Austria* 026/4 Movement plates embossed: BRAUNAU BÖHMEN Year of registration 1902. * former Austrian-Hungarian Danube Federation. Annexed 1920 by Czechoslovakia. The Braunau works operated as independent branch factory. No serial number records are found.	
Addendum: GB 95 Ed. Embossemt. on movemt. 386447	GUSTAV BECKER FREIB.i.SCHL. BRAUNAU i.BOEHM. the number 3, assumed -Braunau-	Addendum:
	NOTE: Additional TRADE MARK data see page.35	Addendum GB-95 Ed.-

TRADEMARK OR TRADENAME MARQUE DE FABRIQUE - NOMS WARENZEICHEN - WORTMARKE	NAMES AND ADDRESSES NOMS ET ADDRESSES NAMEN UND ADDRESSEN	REMARKS OBSERV'TN BEMERKUNG

GUSTAV BECKER
 	
MADE IN BRAUNAU
TSCHECHOSLOVAKIA

	GUSTAV BECKER
	Braunau - Bohemia, former
	Austrian - Hungarian Danube Fed.
	(now Broumov, ČSR)
	Gustav Becker, assembly plant
	since the year 1888. After the
	annexation of Bohemia, year 1918*
	into Czechoslovakia, Becker
	clocks were marketed with stamp:
	    MADE in BRAUNAU
	    TSCHECHOSLOVAKIA
	    -------- 	
	* after World War I
	Note: Serial number index not
	    traceable. Plant closing year
	    unknown.
	BECKER
	
	Clock label, two colour beige
	paper, black and red ink printing
	full size : 4 1/4 x 41/4 inch.
	Note: Original label found year
	1979 at a flea market in London
	England.	

B E C K E R U H R 	Germany Trademark slogan: WOHNKULTUR durch BECKERUHR, (Culture in your living room with a Becker Clock) Registered 26.06.1929, by United Freiburg Clock Factories.	
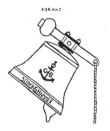	Germany GUSTAV BECKER / SCHWINGHAMMER tradename, registered Gebrueder Junghans A.G. Schramberg 24.01. 1931.	
	GEBRUEDER JUNGHANS A.G. WERK GUSTAV BECKER Schramberg / Black Forest Germany Registered 14.02.1936, manufacturer of clocks made by Junghans, but sold under the GUSTAV BECKER label	

REMARKS OBSERV'TN BEMERKUNG	NAMES AND ADDRESSES NOMS ET ADDRESSES NAMEN UND ADDRESSEN	TRADEMARK OR TRADENAME MARQUE DE FABRIQUE - NOMS WARENZEICHEN - WORTMARKE
	VEREINIGTE FREIBURGER (1) UHRENFABRIKEN A.G. (2) Freiburg, Schlesien (3) (4) Germany (1) United Freiburg (2) Clockfactory -Stockholder Co. (3) Freiburg (now Swiebozice) Poland (4) Silesia (former part of Germany-since 1945 Poland) Was Germany Further literature: UNITED FREIBURG CLOCK FACTORIES, Ltd. by Antique Clock Publishing, Concord, California USA- 94521. © Karl Kochmann,(out of print)	 [1]VEREINIGTE FREIBURGER [2]UHRENFABRIKEN A.G.
	VEREINGTE FREIBURGER UHRENFABRIKEN A.G.,vorm. GUSTAV BECKER * Freiburg-Silesia Germany (now Poland) Trademark registered 14.May 1901 * UNITED FREIBURG CLOCK/WATCH FACTORIES Stockholder Corp. former GUSTAV BECKER Works.	[1]V E R E I N I G T E [3]F R E I B U R G E R [2]U H R E N F A B R I K.
	VEREINIGTE FREIBURGER UHRENFABRIKEN A.G. inclusive former Gustav Becker Works. Freiburg - Silesia Germany (now Poland) Trademark registration: BECKER 01.21. 1905 .	
	VEREINIGTE FREIBURGER UHENFABRIKEN Germany DOMGONG, tradename and trademark registered 02.08.1907.	
	VEREINIGTE FREIBURGER UHRENFABRIKEN A.G. Germany UNIVERSAL, tradename and trademark registered 06.10.1904.	

NOTE: Additional Trademark data see
      page 35

REMARKS OBSERV'TN BEMERKUNG	NAMES AND ADDRESSES NOMS ET ADDRESSES NAMEN UND ADDRESSEN	TRADEMARK OR TRADENAME MARQUE DE FABRIQUE - NOMS WARENZEICHEN - WORTMARKE

GUSTAV BECKER ENTERPRISE, SERIAL NUMBER INDEX - MISC. DATA

YEAR	SERIAL NUMBER	REMARKS
1850	480	
1860	4,000	
1863	10,000	
1865	15,000	
1867	25,000	
1872	50,000	
1875	100,000	From here on: MEDAILLE d'OR *(French)* GOLDEN MEDAL
1880	260,000	
1885	500,000	
1890	800,000	
1892	1,000,000	
1900	1,500,000	From 1899 on: UNITED FREIBURG CLOCK FACTORIES
1913	1,850,000	Full production of clocks limited during World War I (1914-1918)
1923	1,860,000	
1925	1,945,399	Number found on a 2 weight wall clock with attached invoice, dated year 1925
1926	2,244,868	Number found on a hall clock, invoice dated 1926. UNITED FREIBURG CLOCK FACTORIES merged with JUNGHANS
1927 till 1935		Clock production within the JUNGHANS organisation, numbering index not tracable, it is assumed that the index was lost during World War II (1939-1945)
	Braunau works	Numbering index-or system not tracable.
Hennig Archive Dresden - GDR		

GUSTAV BECKER

WORK FORCE

COMPARISION of CLOCK PRODUCTION
--- GUSTAV BECKER ---
-- UNITED FREIBURG CLOCK FACTORIES --

Year	Number of Employees	Annual Production
☆ 1850	☆ Gustav Becker 15	480
☆ 1860	Works 50	4,000
☆ 1870	300	24,000
☆ 1880	500	120,000
☆ 1890	800	105,000
1900	1,400	120,000
1913	2,300	350,000
1923	2,050	360,000

Note: Data compiled "DEUTSCHE UHRMACHER ZEITUNG" (year 1924)

REMARKS OBSERV'TN BEMERKUNG	NAMES AND ADDRESS NOMS ET ADDRESSE NAMEN UND ADDRESSE	TRADEMARK OR TRADENAME MARQUE DE FABRIQUE - NOMS WARENZEICHEN - WORTMARKE
	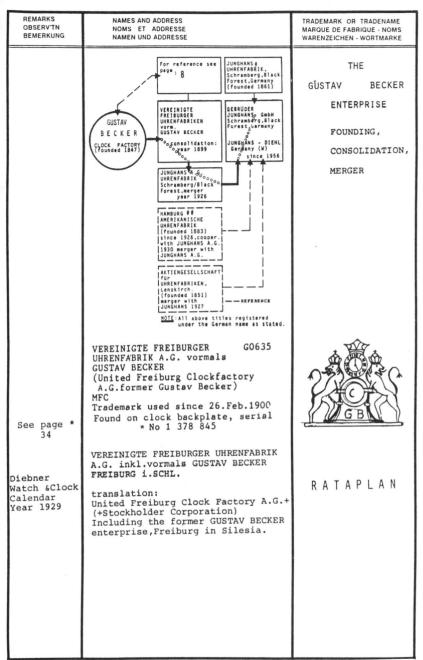	THE GUSTAV BECKER ENTERPRISE FOUNDING, CONSOLIDATION, MERGER
See page * 34 Diebner Watch &Clock Calendar Year 1929	VEREINIGTE FREIBURGER　　G0635 UHRENFABRIK A.G. vormals GUSTAV BECKER (United Freiburg Clockfactory A.G.former Gustav Becker) MFC Trademark used since 26.Feb.1900 Found on clock backplate, serial * No 1 378 845 VEREINIGTE FREIBURGER UHRENFABRIK A.G. inkl.vormals GUSTAV BECKER **FREIBURG i.SCHL.** translation: United Freiburg Clock Factory A.G.+ (+Stockholder Corporation) Including the former GUSTAV BECKER enterprise,Freiburg in Silesia.	RATAPLAN
NOTE:		Addendum GB-95 Ed.-

ADVERTISEMENT
YEAR 1923

photo HENNIG

THE WORLD TRADEMARK (A)
united
FREIBURGER CLOCK FACTORIES
STOCK CORPORATION
incl. former
GUSTAV BECKER
Freiburg Silesia
1800 Worker

GUSTAV BECKER (B)
The Best in Material
Work and Construction

Plate 18

Selection of advertisements published in trade-
journals, newspapers and catalogues of horologica
material suppliers.

Plate 18

Die 300000 ste Beckeruhr

The 300,000 Becker Clock exhibited at the :
Silesia Trade - Industry Fair in the year 1881, in Breslau (now Wroclaw) Poland.
This BECKER - CLOCK was a shining example of the best craftsmanship.
The GUSTAV BECKER enterprise received many awards. The exterior carved out of American Walnut executed by a group of top woodcarver. The location is unknown.

For reference of the 500.000th BECKER CLOCK, called the "BISMARK" see page 38, plate 20.
Page 110, literary essay author SCHMITZ, Reinhard and page 112,
by Callwey - Publication Munich-Germany.
In the year 1892 the Gustav Becker enterprise made the 1,000,000 Clock.

This tall hall clock with a all handcrafted 8 - day Westminster strike move - ment, with musical tuned spiral gongs, temperature compensated plain pendule has survieved rough times, including two World Wars, storage, relocation and protection from pilferage.

The Becker Clock, she is still in Swiebodzice (formerly Freiburg) and keeps perfect time in a factory foreman's office.

Plate 18

Die 1000000 ste Beckeruhr

Plate 19

Description see page 37.

Die 500000 ste Beckeruhr

Plate 20

Description of the "BISMARK CLOCK" see page 39

CHAPTER IV
INTRODUCTION to CATALOGUE PAGES.

Catalogues are as useful data source for horogists, as they were originally used for the sales organization to market clocks worldwide.

The historical - technical publication of the era GUSTAV BECKER's enterprise would be incomplete without examples of well illustrated catalogues, advertisement (*see page 36 , plate 18*), trade publications, and contemporary price lists. Plates shown on the following pages are carefully selected from the author's archives reprinting of entire catalogues was not feasible.

Unless a specific date of publication is noted, data shown on these plates are only approximate.
Styles and design of cases cases continued, and often catalogues data overlapped due production / marketing time. There are still many catalogues in private archiv jealously guarded for variuos personal reason.

Hopefully, the following pages will enable the owner / lover of BECKER clocks to unlock some of its data secrets. This publication shall assist the owner to make a data assesement of its age, model, manufacturer.

Illustrations allow the restorer to restore the clock nearest to the possible original condition. The reproduced pricelists help the collector to gauge its value in relation to its original cost.

☆ ☆ ☆ ☆ ☆

Plate 20
(opposite page 38)

The "BISMARK CLOCK" serial plate number 500,000, another unique markstone of the GUSTAV BECKER enterprise.
Celebrating theier 35th Anniversary, which was also the birthday of the German Chancellor Duke Otto von Bismark (* 1.April 1815 + 30.7.1898), it was also the Birthday month of Gustav Becker.

The 500,000 Gustav Becker clock, therefore was a very fitting Birthday present for the " Iron Chancellor" for his 70th Birthday celebration. Due delays in the course of design and construction, as well the artwork only the drawings could be presented. The clock then was received at a later date by the chancellor.

The famous artist/sculptor Kiefhaber from Magdeburg , Germany was commisioned for the design and supervision of a group of finest artesan woodcarver.
The exterior design theme represents"a walk thru German history . It was fitting to select historical events related to the second part of the 19th century during Otto von Bismark's time, which influenced the course of the Political destiny of Germany under the Emperor WILHELM II of Prussia and the German Empire. Gustav Becker did not live long enough to see the "BISMARK CLOCK" (he passed away in the year 1885).
During Bismark's lifetime, the clock was located in the castle - Friedrichsruh - (Schleswig Holstein, Germany).
The castle suffered extensive damage in the days of WWII but the clock was in time relocated and saved from damage.
The "BISMARK"Clock is now on display in the Bismark Museum* in Friedrichsruh, near Hamburg - Germany
NOTE:*see page 112, essay "Die Bismark Uhr"printed in German.

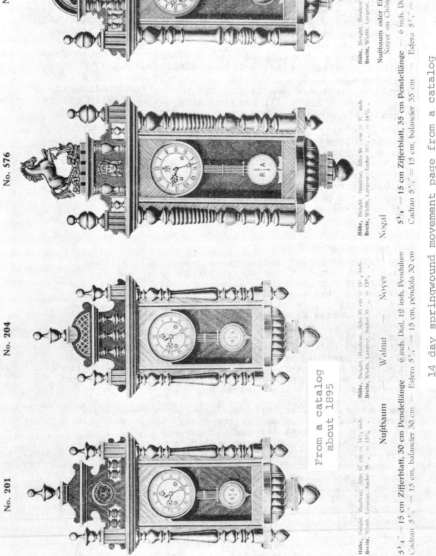

Plate 21 — 14 day springwound movement page from a catalog late 1895. From a catalog about 1895.

From a catalog about 1895

Höhe, Height, Hauteur, Alto 135 cm = 53¼ inch.
Breite, Width, Largeur, Ancho 48 „ = 19 „

Höhe, Height, Hauteur, Alto 135 cm = 53¼ inch.
Breite, Width, Largeur, Ancho 48 „ = 19 „

2 weight "VIENESE" 8 day wall clock with second hand

7" = 18½ cm oder 8" = 21 cm Emaillezifferblatt
7¼ or 8¼ inch. Enamel Dial — Cadran émail 7" = 18½ cm ou 8" = 21 cm
Esfera esmalte 7" = 18½ cm ó 8" = 21 cm

Plate 22

No. 1725   No. 1829

From a catalog about 1895

Höhe, Height, Hauteur, Alto 136 cm = 53½ inch.
Breite, Width, Largeur, Ancho 48 .. = 19 ..

Höhe, Height, Hauteur, Alto 133 cm = 52½ inch.
Breite, Width, Largeur, Ancho 50 .. = 19½ ..

Nußbaum oder Eiche — Walnut or Oak
Noyer ou Chêne — Nogal ó Roble

Nußbaum
Walnut — Noyer — Nogal

2 weight "VIENESE" 8 day wall clock with second hand

7½ or 8¼ inch. Enamel Dial — Cadran émail 7" = 18½ cm ou 8" = 21 cm
Esfera esmalte 7" = 18½ cm ó 8" = 21 cm

Plate 23

No. 3004   No. 3020   No. 3020/27   No. 3018/28

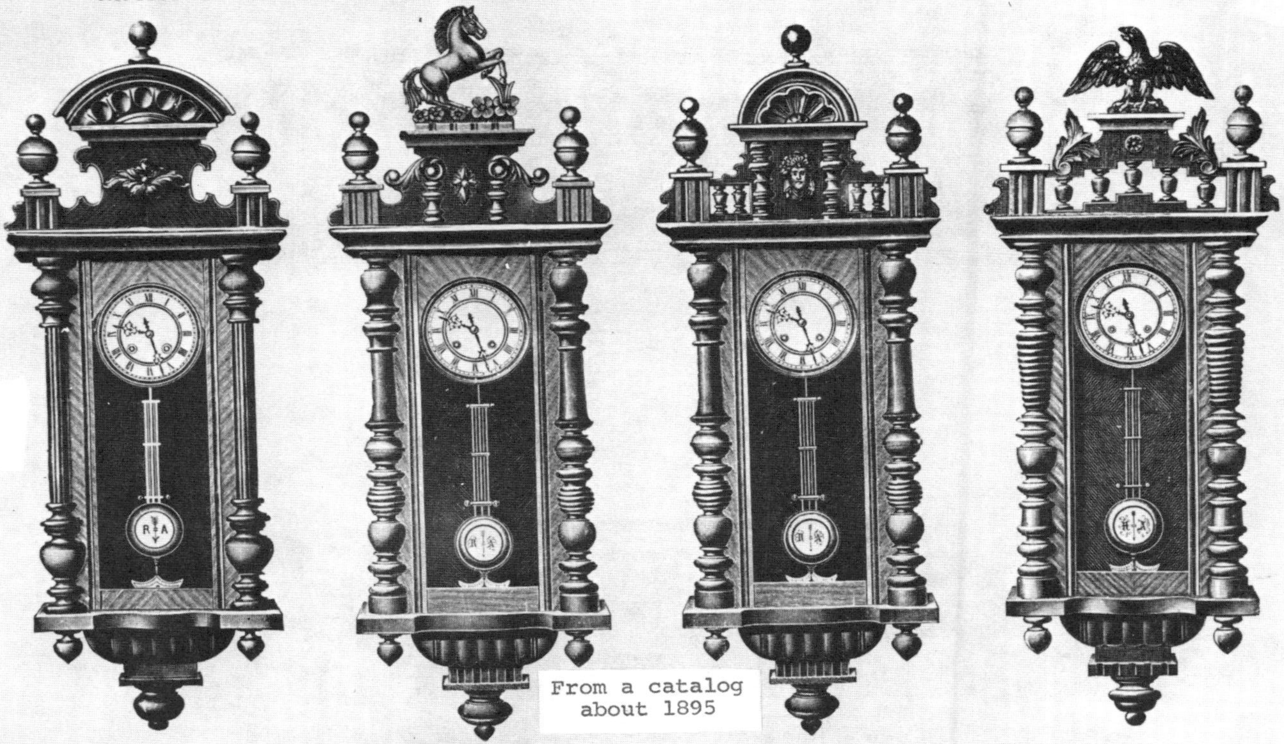

From a catalog about 1895

Höhe, Height, Hauteur, Alto 101 cm = 39½ inch.   **Höhe,** Height, Hauteur, Alto 103 cm = 39½ inch.   **Höhe,** Height, Hauteur, Alto 99 cm = 39 inch.   **Höhe,** Height, Hauteur, Alto 100 cm = 39½ inch.
Breite, Width, Largeur, Ancho 40 „ = 15¾ „   **Breite,** Width, Largeur, Ancho 40 „ = 15¾ „   **Breite,** Width, Largeur, Ancho 40 „ = 15¾ „   **Breite,** Width, Largeur, Ancho 40 „ = 15¾ „

Nußbaum oder Eiche – Walnut or Oak – Noyer ou Chêne – Nogal ó Roble   Nußbaum – Walnut – Noyer – Nogal

5¾" = 15 cm Zifferblatt, 42 cm Pendellänge – 6 inch. Dial, 16½ inch. Pendulum – Cadran 5⁷" = 15 cm, balancier 42 cm – Esfera 5¾" = 15 cm, péndolo 42 cm

14 day springwound movement page from a catalog, year about 1885

Plate 24

No. 1836

No. 1833

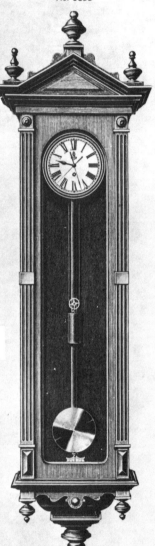

9" = 23½ cm geätztes Silberzifferblatt

9¼ inch. engraved silvered Dial

Cadran argenté et gravé 9" = 23½ cm

Esfera plateada y grabada 9" = 23½ cm

From a catalog about 1895

Höhe, Height, Hauteur, Alto 195 cm = 76¾ inch.
Breite, Width, Largeur, Ancho 58 = 23

Höhe, Height, Hauteur, Alto 192 cm = 74½ inch.
Breite, Width, Largeur, Ancho 55 = 21¾

1 weight 8 day hall regulator silver plated dial - sweeping second hand

Plate 25

From a catalog of the twenties

Höhe, Height, Hauteur, Alto 36 cm = 14¼ inch.
Breite, Width, Largeur, Ancho 26 „ = 10¼ „

Höhe, Height, Hauteur, Alto 49 cm = 19¼ inch.
Breite, Width, Largeur, Ancho 30 „ = 11⅞ „

14 day spring mantle clock half and full hour strike

Blechzifferblatt 14 cm
Lacquered Dial 5½ inch. — Cadran tôle 14 cm — Esfera en lata 14 cm

1 oder 14 Tag Schlagwerk, Tonfeder
1 or 14 Day ordinary Strike — 1 ou 15 jours sonnerie ordinaire
1 ó 15 dias soneria ordinaria

Plate 26

No. 283   No. 284

Höhe, Height, Hauteur, Alto 56 cm = 22 inch.
Breite, Width, Largeur, Ancho 27½ = 10¾

Höhe, Height, Hauteur, Alto 53 cm = 21 inch.
Breite, Width, Largeur, Ancho 29 = 11½

Nußbaum — Walnut — Noyer — Nogal

14 day spring mantle clock. Painted dial half and full hour strike.

Zifferblatt 14 cm
Dial 5½ inch. — Cadran 14 cm — Esfera 14 cm

From a catalog of the twenties

1 oder 14 Tag Schlagwerk, Tonfeder
1 or 14 Day ordinary Strike — 1 ou 15 jours sonnerie ordinaire
1 ó 15 dias soneria ordinaria

Plate 27

No. 336

14 Tag ½ std. Schlagwerk, Tonfeder
14 Day ½ hour ordinary Strike
15 jours à sonnerie ½ h. ordinaire
15 dias sonería ½ h. ordinaria

Silberzifferblatt ☐ 16½ cm
Silvered Dial ☐ 6½ inch.
Cadran argenté ☐ 16½ cm
Esfera plateada ☐ 16½ cm

Höhe, Height, Hauteur, Alto 31½ cm = 13½ inch.
Breite, Width, Largeur, Ancho 20½ „ = 8 „

Mantle clocks with half and full hour strike, all bevelled glass. Silver plated dial – 14 day movement.

No. 329

Höhe, Height, Hauteur, Alto 36 cm = 14½ inch.
Breite, Width, Largeur, Ancho 22½ „ = 9 „

Nußbaum — Walnut
Noyer — Nogal

Silberzifferblatt einschl. Lünette
12½ cm, Bombéglas

Silvered Dial with Bezel 5 inch.,
Convex Glass

Cadran argenté avec Lunette
12½ cm, Verre bombé

Esfera plateada con Aro 12½ cm,
Vidrio convexo

Facettegläser in Messingfassung
Bevelled Glasses in Brass setting
Verres biseautés sertis en laiton
Cristales biselados engastados en latón

From a catalog of the twenties

No. 340

Höhe, Height, Hauteur, Alto 36 cm = 14½ inch.
Breite, Width, Largeur, Ancho 22½ „ = 9 „

Nußbaum od. Eiche — Walnut or Oak
Noyer ou Chêne — Nogal ó Roble

Plate 28

No. 291

Höhe, Height, Hauteur, Alto 25½ cm = 10 inch.
Breite, Width, Largeur, Ancho 50 . = 19¾ .

No. 5   From a catalog of the twenties   No. 5

Höhe, Height, Hauteur, Alto 27½ cm = 10¾ inch.   Höhe, Height, Hauteur, Alto 33 cm = 13 inch.   Höhe, Height, Hauteur, Alto 27½ cm = 10¾ inch.
Breite, Width, Largeur, Ancho 21 . = 8¼ .   Breite, Width, Largeur, Ancho 21 . = 8¼ .   Breite, Width, Largeur, Ancho 21 . = 8¼ .

Messinggehäuse mattgold oder Altmessing
Brass Case gilt or antique Brass — Boîte laiton doré mat ou laiton antique
Caja de latón dorado mate ó latón viejo

14 day decor mantle clock, case brass - satin gold finish or antique brass case - silver plated dial half and full hour strike.

Plate 29

No. 361

Eiche
ak — Chêne
Roble

Silberzifferblatt einschl.
Lünette 14 cm, Bombéglas

Silvered Dial with Bezel
5½ inch., Convex Glass

Cadran argenté avec Lunette
14 cm, Verre bombé

Esfera plateada con Aro
14 cm, Vidrio convexo

Höhe, Height, Hauteur, Alto 24½ cm = 9½ inch.
Breite, Width, Largeur, Ancho 34 „ = 13½ „

No. 364

Eiche
ak — Chêne
Roble

Silberzifferblatt einschl.
Lünette 14 cm, Bombéglas

Silvered Dial with Bezel
5½ inch., Convex Glass

Cadran argenté avec Lunette
14 cm, Verre bombé

Esfera plateada con Aro
14 cm, Vidrio convexo

Höhe, Height, Hauteur, Alto 24 cm = 9½ inch.
Breite, Width, Largeur, Ancho 32½ „ = 12¾ „

Mantle clocks with
half and full hour
strike, all
bevelled glass.
Silver plated dial -
14 day movement.

No. 348

Eiche
 — Chêne
Roble

Silberzifferblatt einschl.
Lünette 14 cm, Bombéglas

Silvered Dial with Bezel
5½ inch., Convex Glass

Cadran argenté avec Lunette
14 cm, Verre bombé

Esfera plateada con Aro
14 cm, Vidrio convexo

Höhe, Height, Hauteur, Alto 23 cm = 9 inch.
Breite, Width, Largeur, Ancho 39 „ = 15½ „

Plate 30

No. 444
Facetteglas — Bevelled Glass
Verre biseauté — Cristal biselado

Geätztes Silberzifferblatt
21×16 cm

Engraved silvered Dial
8¼×6½ inch.

Cadran argenté et gravé
21×16 cm

Esfera plateada y grabada
21×16 cm

From a catalog of the twenties

Höhe, Height, Hauteur, Alto 33 cm = 13 inch.
Breite, Width, Largeur, Ancho 27½ „ = 10¾ „

Westminster chime mantle clock 8 day movement. Silver plated fac
model 444 see page 73 for details of movement.

No. 443

No. 437

Silberzifferblatt einschl. mass. Lünette 17 cm, bombiertes Facetteglas

Silvered Dial with solid Bezel 6¾ inch., Convex bevelled Glass

Cadran argenté avec Lunette massive 17 cm, Verre biseauté et bombé

Esfera plateada con Aro macizo 17 cm, Cristal convexo y biselado

Höhe, Height, Hauteur, Alto 34½ cm = 13½ inch.
Breite, Width, Largeur, Ancho 27 „ = 10½ „

Eiche — Oak — Chêne — Roble

Höhe, Height, Hauteur, Alto 38 cm = 15 inch.
Breite, Width, Largeur, Ancho 27 „ = 10½ „

Eiche mit Intarsien
Oak inlaid — Chêne avec marqueterie
Roble con labor embutido

Plate 31

No. 428

Höhe, Height, Hauteur, Alto 27½ cm = 10⅞ inch.
Breite, Width, Largeur, Ancho 56 „ = 22 „

Westminster mantle clock 8 day movement. Silver plated face.

From a catalog of the twenties

No. 423

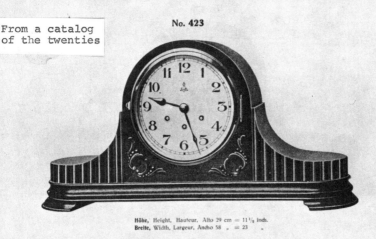

Höhe, Height, Hauteur, Alto 29 cm = 11⅜ inch.
Breite, Width, Largeur, Ancho 58 „ = 23 „

Eiche — Oak — Chêne — Roble

Silberzifferblatt einschl. Lünette 19½ cm, Bombéglas
Silvered Dial with Bezel 7¾ inch., Convex Glass — Cadran argenté avec Lunette 19½ cm, Verre bombé
Esfera plateada con Aro 19½ cm, Vidrio convexo

14 Tag ½ std. Schlagwerk auf Gong
14 Day ½ hour Gong Strike — 15 jours sonnerie ½ h. sur Gong — 15 dias soneria ½ h. sobre Gong

Plate 32

No. 557
Glattes Glas Plain Glass
Verre plat Vidrio ordinario

No. 558
3 Facettegläser 3 Bevelled Glasses
3 Verres biseautés 3 Cristales biselados

Höhe, Height, Hauteur, Alto 57 cm = 22½ inch.
Breite, Width, Largeur, Ancho 27 „ = 10⅝".

Nußbaumfarbig oder Eiche
Walnut Colour or Oak
Façon Noyer ou Chêne
Color Nogal ó Roble

No. 563

Höhe, Height, Hauteur, Alto 58 cm = 23 inch.
Breite, Width, Largeur, Ancho 27 „ = 10⅝".

Nußbaum Walnut Noyer Nogal

No. 559

Höhe, Height, Hauteur, Alto 62 cm = 24½ inch.
Breite, Width, Largeur, Ancho 27½ „ = 10⅞".

Nußbaumfarbig oder Eiche
Walnut Colour or Oak
Façon Noyer ou Chêne

No. 540
Glattes Glas Plain Glass
Verre plat Vidrio ordinario

No. 560
3 Facettegläser 3 Bevelled Glasses
3 Verres biseautés 3 Cristales biselados

Höhe, Height, Hauteur, Alto 62 cm = 24½ inch.
Breite, Width, Largeur, Ancho 27½ „ = 10⅞".

Nußbaumfarbig, Eiche od. Mahagonifarbig
Walnut Colour, Oak or Mahogany Colour
Façon Noyer, Chêne ou Façon Acajou
Nogal, Roble ó color Caoba

From a catalog of the twenties

Typical home wall clock. 14 day spring movement. Half

No. 3612	No. 3614
Facettegläser — Bevelled Glasses	Facettegläser — Bevelled Glasses
Verres biseautés — Cristales biselados	Verres biseautés — Cristales biselados

From a catalog of the twenties

Höhe, Height, Hauteur, Alto 78 cm = 30⅞ inch.
Breite, Width, Largeur, Ancho 34 = 13½

Höhe, Height, Hauteur, Alto 76½ cm = 30⅛ inch.
Breite, Width, Largeur, Ancho 34½ = 13½

Eiche
Oak — Chêne — Roble

Nußbaum oder Eiche
Walnut or Oak — Noyer ou Chêne — Nogal ó Roble

Parlor wall clock. 14 day spring movement with all bevelled glass door framed in brass molding.

Plate 34

From a catalog of the twenties

No. 4769
Facettegläser in Messingfassung
Bevelled Glasses in Brass setting
Verres biseautés sertis en laiton
Cristales biselados engastados en latón

No. 4768
Facetteglas — Bevelled Glass
Verre biseauté — Cristal biselado

Höhe, Height, Hauteur, Alto 75 cm = 29½ inch.
Breite, Width, Largeur, Ancho 34 „ = 13½ „

Höhe, Height, Hauteur, Alto 76 cm = 30 inch.
Breite, Width, Largeur, Ancho 36 „ = 14¼ „

Parlor wall clock. 14 day spring movement with all bevelled glass door framed in brass molding.

8" = 21 cm **Silberzifferblatt**
8¼ inch. silvered Dial — Cadran argenté 8" = 21 cm — Esfera plateada 8" = 21 cm

Plate 35

No. 1871
Facettegläser — Bevelled Glasses
Verres biseautés — Cristales biselados

No. 1877
Facettegläser — Bevelled Glasses
Verres biseautés — Cristales biselados

No. 1878
Facettegläser in Messingfassung
Bevelled Glasses in Brass setting
Verres biseautés sertis en laiton
Cristales biselados engastados en latón

From a catalog of the twenties

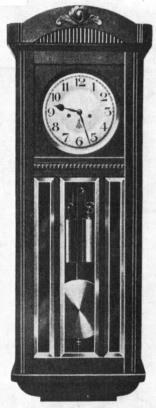

Höhe, Height, Hauteur, Alto 98 cm = 38½ inch.
Breite, Width, Largeur, Ancho 35 = 13¾

Höhe, Height, Hauteur, Alto 95½ cm = 37½ inch.
Breite, Width, Largeur, Ancho 36 = 14½

Nußbaum oder Eiche — Walnut or Oak
Noyer ou Chêne — Nogal ó Roble

Eiche — Oak
Chêne — Roble

8" = 21 cm Silberzifferblatt
8¼ inch. silvered Dial — Cadran argenté 8" = 21 cm — Esfera plateada 8" = 21 cm

2 weight parlor clock. 8 day movement strike half and full hour. All bevelled glass door.

Plate 36

Grandfather Clocks — Full ⁴/₄ Westminster Chime

No. 2582
Glattes Glas — Plain Glass
Verre plat — Vidrio plano

No. 2596

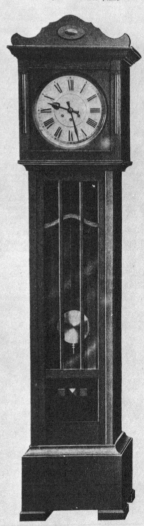

From a catalog of the twenties

Eiche
Oak — Chêne — Roble

No. 2582

Garn. No. 9, 10" =
27 cm Silberzifferblatt

Silvered Dial 10 ¼ inch.
Cadran argenté 27 cm
Esfera plateada 27 cm

No. 2596

Garn. No. 524 =
Messingzifferblatt 26×26 cm
mit aufgelegten Gußverzierungen
und aufgelegtem, geätztem Silberzahlenreif

10 ¼" Square Brass mounted Dial
with solid Brass Corners 8" silvered
Circle

Cadran cuivre 26×26 cm

8 day spring movement meduim size grandfather clock.

Höhe, Height, Hauteur, Alto 186 cm = 73 inch.
Breite, Width, Largeur, Ancho 44 „ = 17 ¼ „

Höhe, Height, Hauteur, Alto 178 cm = 70 inch.
Breite, Width, Largeur, Ancho 43 „ = 17 „

Plate 37

No. 2663

Facetteglas — Bevelled Glass
Verre biseauté — Cristal biselado

No. 2668

Facetteglas — Bevelled Glass
Verre biseauté — Cristal biselado

From a catalog of the twenties

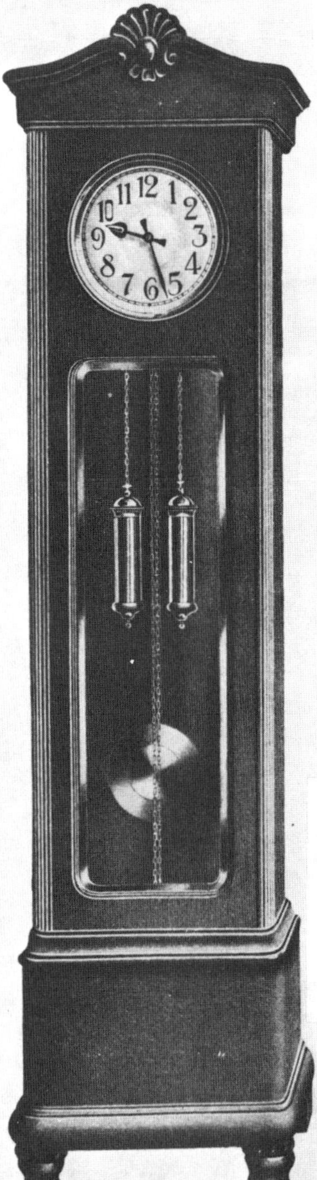

No. 2663

Eiche, Nußbaum oder Mahagoni poliert

Oak, Walnut or polished Mahogany

Chêne, Noyer ou Acajou poli

Roble, Nogal ó Caoba pulida

Garn. No. 158, 10" = 27 cm Silberzifferblatt

Silvered Dial 10¾ inch.

Cadran argenté 27 cm

Esfera plateada 27 cm

No. 2668

Mahagoni poliert

Polished Mahogany

Acajou poli

Caoba pulida

Garn. No. 2643

8 day weight hall grandfather clock. Half and full hour strike BIM BAM rod gong.

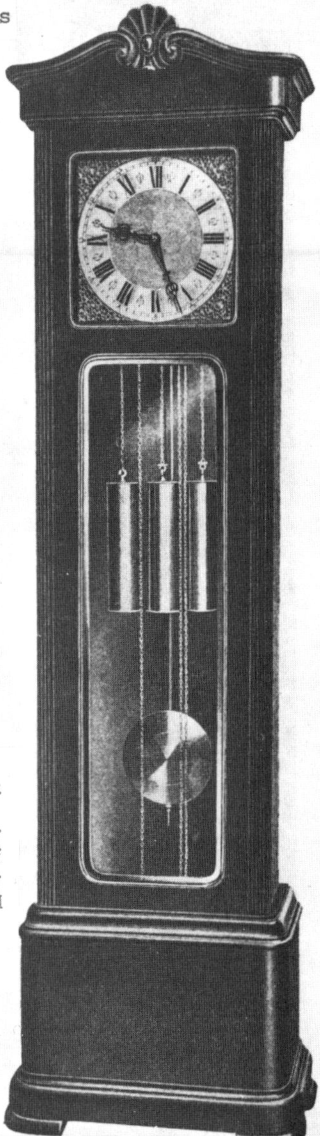

Höhe, Height. Hauteur. Alto 206 cm = 81 inch.
Breite, Width. Largeur. Ancho 56 „ = 22 „

Höhe, Height. Hauteur. Alto 201 cm = 79½ inch.
Breite, Width. Largeur. Ancho 56 „ = 22 „

Plate 38

No. 2678
Facetteglas — Bevelled Glass
Verre biseauté — Cristal biselado

No. 2666
Facetteglas — Bevelled Glass
Verre biseauté — Cristal biselado

Eiche — Oak
Chêne — Roble

Garn. No. 151, 12" = 31½ cm
Silberzifferblatt

8 day westminster hall grandfather clock, silver decor plated facering with brass cast decor.

From a catalog of the twenties

Höhe, Height, Hauteur, Alto 202 cm = 79¾ inch.
Breite, Width, Largeur, Ancho 53 = 21

Höhe, Height, Hauteur, Alto 200 cm = 79 inch.
Breite, Width, Largeur, Ancho 62 = 24½

Plate 39

Mahagoni poliert mit Intarsien, Facetteglas
Polished Mahogany inlaid with Bevelled Glass — Acajou poli avec marqueterie, verre biseauté
Caoba pulida con labor embutido, cristal biselado

No. 2586

Ia 8 Tag Federzug ⁴/₄ Schlagwerk
mit Westminstergong

Garn. No. 2586 = 37 × 26 cm
fein geätztes Silberzifferblatt
mit aufgelegten Gußverzierungen

8 Day solid ⁴/₄ Spring Movement Westminster Chime Silvered and engraved Dial 14 ¹/₂ × 10 ¹/₄ inch.

Mouvement massif à ressort ⁴/₄ Carillon Westminster Cadran argenté et gravé 37 × 26 cm

Máquina con muelle fina maciza ⁴/₄ 8 dias de cuerda Carillón Westminster Esfera plateada y grabada 37 × 26 cm

From a catalog
of the twenties

No. 2588

Ia 8 Tag Kettenzug ⁴/₄ Schlagwerk, 3 Lauf, mit Westminstergong, od. kombiniert Whittington- und Westminstergong

Garn. No. 2588 = 37 × 26 cm
schweres Messingzifferblatt
mit aufgelegten Gußverzierungen, aufgelegtem Silberzahlenreifen mit aufgelegten goldfarbigen Zahlen

English style hall clock. With 8 day spring, or 8 day weight movement. Face hand etched and engraved. Bevelled glass door selective Westminster or Withington chimes. Case all mahagony with elaborate inlaid work.

Höhe, Height, Hauteur, Alto 195 cm = 76³/₄ inch.
Breite, Width, Largeur, Ancho 47 „ = 18¹/₂ „

Plate 40

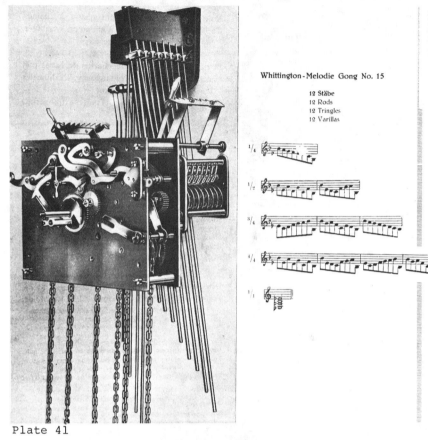

Plate 41

The Westminster Chimes melody comes from "Big Ben," The clock installed in the tower of Westminster Palace, London, in 1859. The composition itself is from G.F.Handel's oratorio, "The Messiah," Movement No. 45, " I know that My Redeemer Liveth," written in 1741.

The Whittington and St.Michael Chimes also have English origins. The lengendary Richard Whittington, 1358?-1423, rose from poverty to become Lord Mayor of London.

The melody of the bells is derived from the church of St. Mary's-La Bow in Cheapside, London. The story goes that when the runaway "Dick" heard the chimes of St. Mary's, he turned around and returned to London, and later served three terms as Lord Mayor of the city.

The bells for St. Michael's Church in Charleston, South Carolina, came from London. However, after the British captured the city in 1780 during the Revolutionary War, the soldiers sent them back to England as a booty. In 1867, The American church had a new set of bells cast from the old molds with the inscription, "Home again, home again from foreign land."

CHAPTER V
HISTORICAL CATALOGUE DATA.

The following pages are a selection of historical pages from Catalogue No. 125 of the UNITED FREIBURG CLOCK FACTORY-GUSTAV BECKER WORKS, Freiburg, published in 1925.

Co-author Hennig chose the pages of the pricelist as the most representative. Please note that the publication date is not necessarily the year the factory introduced the model.
It may have appeared up to one year previous.

Plate 00

    Prices quoted are in gold-backed Reichsmarks, issued following the great inflation of the early 1920s.
They are not intended as a guide to today's value for any BECKER CLOCK. In comparison, the price of gold in the United States of America from 1837 to 1933 was $ 20.67 a troy ounce.

    As an estimate of the price of a clock in relation to the cost of living, the top wages for a scilled craftsman workung a 5½-day, 48-50 hour week, were 16 to 25 RM a day, or about 350 RM to 550 RM a month. A white collar employee earned about 380 RM monthly.

    Earlier catalogues and records are not available. Much disappeared following mergers and reorganizations, and especially in upheavals during and after World War II. The remaining files in Swiebodzice Poland (Formerly Freiburg, Silesia) are not accessible - and or destroyed - since having no record value for the present occupants of the former Becker factory.

NUMERICAL - INDEX
Nummern-Verzeichnis.

① Model Nr.	② Page Seite	① Model Nr.	② Page Seite	① Model Nr.	② Page Seite	① Model Nr.	② Page Seite
5—88	2	510—527	9	1250—1260	6	2062—2073	4
130—198	5	541—564 **65**	12	1269—1280	15	2302	8
201—204	9	576—582	9	1462—1474	7	③ 2621—2686 NA	18
211—284 **64**	7	592—593	12	1554—1829	10	3004—3020	9
③ 290—444 NA	8	601—669	2	1833—1836	19	3111—3746 NA	14
445—455 NA	6	700—760	3	1846—1900 **66**	10	4001—4002	9
461—503 NA	7	901—952	3—4	1962—1973	4	4111—4878 NA	14
508	6	③ 1174—1188 NA	7	1983	18	5001—5002	9

④ Allgemeine Bemerkungen.

⑤**Bestellungen:** Durch die Uhren-Großhandlungen erbeten.
Bei Bestellungen empfiehlt es sich, zur Vermeidung von zeitraubenden Rückfragen die Nummer und Holzart der Gehäuse, die Werksorte und die Gongart der einzelnen Muster, in Uebereinstimmung mit den in unseren Katalogen und Preislisten gebrauchten Nummern und Bezeichnungen genau anzugeben.

⑥**Eichengehäuse roh und gefärbt:** Eichengehäuse kommen nur in „roh", d. h. ungebeizt zum Lager und werden, wenn bei Bestellung keinerlei Farbe vermerkt ist, in „roh" geliefert. Bezüglich der Eichenholzfarbe gilt: Eiche 1 : roh;
Eiche 2: hell gebeizt. Eiche 8: mittel geräuch. Eiche 10: hellbraun geräuch. Eiche 14: dunkelbr. geräuch.
„ 3: mittel geb. „ 9: hellbraun geb. „ 13: Kaffeebraun geb. „ 16: schwarzbraun geb.
Die Preise für Eiche verstehen sich, wo nicht anders vermerkt, für Eiche gebeizt nach Nr. 2—16 der Farbenskala 1925.

⑦**Originalkisten enthalten:**
50 Reisewecker od. 50 Wanduhrwerke. 24 Runduhren 6—9" od. Einsatzuhren. 12 Regulateure 5³/₄".
50, 60 oder 100 Wecker wie Baby. 12 „ 10—12". 6 „ 7" oder 8".
50 Holzwecker Nr. 1962—1973. 12 Tischuhren Nr. 329—369. 18 kleine moderne Wanduhren.
24 Küchen- oder Marineuhren. 6 „ Nr. 408—444. 12 moderne Wanduhren.
12 Jahresuhren. 18 Regulateure Nr. 511—582. 6 „ über 80 cm Höhe.

⑤ Orders: Thru wholesale outlets appreciated.
We recommand, to assure speedy handling
of your orders,that you specify,number,
type of wood of the case,the type of gong
in accordance with our catalogue code.
⑥ Oak clock case unfinished and stained: Oak cases
will be only "unfinished"shipped,in case
your order does not specify the color.
Oak 1=unfinished;Oak 2:light stained,
3:medium stained,oak 8:medium smoked,
9:light stained ,oak 10:light smoked,
13:Coffee brown, oak 14:dark brown smoked,
16:black-brown stained.
⑦ Original shipping container :
50 alarm clocks or wall clock movements
24 Kitchen-or marine clocks, or 12 anniversary clocks.
24 Round clocks 6-9" diam.,12 round clocks 10-12" diam.
12 Mantle clocks No.329-369,6 mantle clocks No.408-444,
18 Regulator No.511-582,or 12 regulator 5 3/4"diam.
6 Regulator 7" Or 8" diam.18 small modern wall clocks,
or 12 modern wall clocks,or 6 modern wall clocks over
32" high.

① Model No.refers to page No.
② Refer to page No.(BOLD)
③ Pricelist not avialable
④ General remarks

Plate 42

Katal.-Seite 38—39	ROUND WALL CLOCKS **Runduhren** mit 14 Tag **Pendelgang**-Werken Werke-Abbildungen Katalog N. 5, Seite 36 u. 88	DIAMETER	6"	7"	8"	9"	10"	12"
		Durchm. des Rahmens:	28 cm	30½ cm	33½ cm	37½ cm	40 cm	45 cm
		Durchm. des Zifferbl.:	16 „	18½ „	21 „	23½ „	26 „	31½ „
			Gehwerk	Gehwerk	Gehwerk	Gehwerk	Gehwerk	Gehwerk
	14 Tag Gehwerk mit Hohltrieben Werk Sag. H.		14 DAY MOVEMENT					
445	Nußbaumfarbig oder schwarz Walnut or black		16,75	17,25	18,—	18,50	20,50	25,—
	Buche hell Buxwood light		17,25	17,75	18,50	19,25	21,25	25,75
449 G	Nußbaumfarbig Walnut like stain or black		19,50	20,—	21,50	23,50	26,—	30,—
	Buche hell Buxwood light . . .		20,—	20,50	22,—	24,25	26,75	30,75
		Durchm. des Rahmens:	29 cm	32½ cm	35½ cm	39½ cm	42½ cm	49 cm
		Durchm. des Zifferbl.:	16 „	18½ „	21 „	23½ „	26½ „	31½ „
455 u. 455 a	Nußbaumfarbig Walnut or black und Lackblatt		20,50	21,50	23,25	25,75	28,50	32,75
	Buche hell oder mahagonifarbig Buxwood light or mahagoni stain		21,—	22,—	23,75	26,50	29,25	33,50
446	Nußbaumfarbig oder schwarz mit fl. Glas und Lackblatt Walnut wood, oak or black with glass and laquer face.		—	—	—	—	—	31,—
	Buche hell oder mahagonifarbig		—	—	—	—	—	31,75
450 u. 450 a	Echt Nußbaum, Eiche oder schwarz mit Glas und Lackblatt . .		26,—	26,75	29,—	32,25	34,50	37,25

Extra charges for variation in movements:
Mehrpreise für andere Werksorten:

Sag. 14 Tag Gehw. „Silesia" mit massiven Trieben	Ag. Ia. 14 Tag massiv Gehwerk	Spiralgong	Sa. H. 14 Tag Schlagwerk mit Hohltrieben	Rodgong No. 2	Sa. H. R. 14 Tag Rechenschlagwerk mit Hohltrieben	Spiralgong	Sa. 14 Tag Schlagwerk „Silesia" mit massiven Trieben	Rodgong No. 2	Sa. R. 14 Tag Rechenschlagwerk „Silesia" mit massiven Trieben
			Tonleder	Gong Nr. 2	Tonleder		Tonleder	Gong Nr. 2	Tonleder Gong Nr. 2
0,75	5,50		5,50	7,—	6,50	8,—	6,75	8,25	7,75 9,25
			14 day strike with latern gears		14 day strike with latern gears		14 day strike with full stock gears "Silesia"		14 day rack strike "Silesia" with full stock gears

Katal.-Seite	№	OFFICE WALL CLOCKS **Kontoruhren** Werke-Abbildungen Katalog Nr. 5, Seite 36 u. 88 Oong- „ „ „ 5,' „ 88	Sag. H. 14 Tag Gehwerk mit Hohltrieb.	Sag. 14 Tag Gehwerk „Silesia" mit mass. Trieben	Ag. 14 Tag Gehwerk massiv	Sa. H. 14 Tag Schlagw. Hohltrieb. Gloriag. Nr. 2	Sa. 14 Tag Schlagw. „Silesia" mit mass. Trieben Gloriag. Nr. 2	Sa. 8 Tag Schlagw. „Silesia" mass. Triebe Svong. Nr. 3/9 bimbam
40	446	siehe oben						
„	447	Nußbaum oder Eiche gebeizt	57,—	57,75	62,50	64,50	65,75	—
42	508	„ „ „ „ „	31,50	32,25	37,—	39,—	40,25	—
41	1250	Eiche gebeizt	41,25	42,—	46,75	48,75	50,—	55,—
„	1251		44,50	45,25	50,—	52,—	53,25	58,25
„	1260	Nußbaum	23,75	24,50	29,25	31,25	32,50	—
„	1260	Eiche gebeizt	25,25	26,—	30,75	32,75	34,—	—

R. Rechenschlagwerk erhöht um: 1,— gegen Werk **Sa. H.** und **Sa.** Eiche roh weniger: 1,25

Plate 43

SHIP CLOCKS

Katalog-Seite 43—46	Schiffsuhren mit 8 Tag constant Anker-Gehwerk Cg. Werk-Abbildung Katalog Nr. 5, Seite 43				Katalog-Seite 44—45	Barometer Ia. Qualität Barometer-Werk			
№	462	463	464	472	№	462 B	463 B	464 B	472 B
	46,75	56,75	56,75	45,75		35,—	45,—	45,—	34,—

№ 461 Starkes solides Messinggehäuse, Messing poliert, vernickelt oder schwarz oxydiert, geätztes Silberzifferblatt mit Werk M. I. = Ia. massiv 8 Tag Gehwerk, ff. Anker-Echappement . . . . 120,—

ILLUSTRATIONS NOT AVAILABLE

ANNIVERSARY CLOCKS
Jahresuhren

Katalog-Seite 47—48	№	476 mit Glasglocke	479 mit Glasglocke	503 mit Glasglocke	481 Messinggehäuse
		43,—	46,—	49,—	100,—

Verpackung der Glasglocken in extra Kistchen pro Stück 1,—

Schreibtisch-Uhren mit 8 Tag Anker-Gehwerk Ra.
Desk clocks with 8 day anchor escapement movement.

Preise der Einsteckwerke Ra. siehe Seite 2 dieser Liste

Katalog-Seite 50—54	New mod №	1174	1175	1178	1179	1181	1183	1188	1462 New model No.
	alte №	211	212	214	215	216	217	213	231 Old Model No.
		15,50	15,50	18,25	18,25	18,25	18,25	16,25	20,50
	New model No.			Walnut or mahogani stained		Oak		Walnut or mahogani stained	
	1464 Eiche	1464 Nußb.- od. mahagonifarbig		1467 Eiche	1467 Nußb.- od. mahagonifarbig				
	alte №	232	232	"	"	233	233	"	"
	Old Model No.	20,50		23,—		21,50		24,90	
	New model No. №	1469	1470	1471	1472	1473	1474		
	alte №	234	235	236	237	—	—		
		23,50	26,75	26,75	23,75	23,75	20,—		

COTTAGE CLOCKS
Cottage Tischuhren
Werke-Abbildungen Katalog Nr. 5, Seite 78 und 88

Katalog-Seite	№		I. S. 1 Tag amerikan. Schlagwerk Tonfeder	14 day american strike-spiral-gong 14 Tag amerikan. Schlagwerk Tonfeder
56	281/45	Nußbaumfarbig poliert Walnut stained-polished	22,—	27,50
"	282/45	" " "	23,—	28,50
57	283/46	" " "	24,—	29,50
"	284/46	" " "	25,—	30,50

the BOLD printed number refers to the page of this publication.

Plate 44

Katalog-Seite	№	MODERN WALLCLOCKS **Moderne Wanduhren** Werk-Abbildungen Katalog Nr. 5, Seite 88 Gong-Abbildungen „ Nr. 5, „ 88/89	Sa. H. 14 Tag Schlagwerk mit Hohltrieben ① Tonfeder	② Gloriagong Nr. 2	③ Domgong Nr. 4	Harfengong Nr. 5 Svengong 8 Tag bim-bam Nr. 3/9	8 Tag Triogong bim-bam Nr. 9	D. R. 8 Tag massiv 3/4 Schlagwerk Universalgong Nr. 1
						④	⑤	⑥
92	541	Walnut or oak stained Nußbaumfarbig oder Eiche gebeizt	41,50	43,50	—	ILLUSTRATIONS NOT AVAILABLE		
„	548	Walnut style stained Nußbaumfarbig	34,—	36,—	—	—	—	—
„	549	Walnut or oak stained Nußbaumfarbig oder Eiche gebeizt	35,—	37,—	—	—	—	—
93	540/52	„ „ „ „	37,50	39,50	41,50	44,50	45,—	60,50
„	„	Mahagoni style stained Mahagonifarbig	47,50	49,50	51,50	54,50	55,—	70,50
„	557/52	Walnut or oak stained Nußbaumfarbig oder Eiche gebeizt The BOLD printed number refers to the page of this publication	35,50	37,50	—	—	—	—
„	558/52		37,75	39,75	—	—	—	—
„	559/52	„ „ „ „	36,50	38,50	40,50	43,50	44,—	59,50
„	560/52	„ „ „ „	40,—	42,—	44,—	47,—	47,50	63,—
„	„	Mahagonifarbig	50,—	52,—	54,—	57,—	57,50	73,—
„	563/52	Walnut Nußbaum	36,50	38,50	—	—	—	—
94	564	Oak stained Eiche gebeizt	38,—	40,—	42,—	45,—	45,50	61,—
„	592	Nußbaumfarbig oder Eiche gebeizt	44,—	46,—	48,—	51,—	51,50	67,—
„	593	„ „ „ „	46,50	48,50	50,50	53,50	54,—	69,50

Eiche roh ermäßigt gegen Eiche gebeizt bei Nr. 541, 549, 557/58 1,25
Discount for unfinished oak clock cases   „ Nr. 540, 559, 560, 564, 592/93 1,50

Gong 2 a am Tragstuhl gegen Tonfeder mehr: 1,50
Universalgong Nr. 1 gegen Tonfeder mehr: Universal gong 2,50

Werk Sa. 14 Tag Schlagwerk „Silesia" mit massiven Trieben gegen Werk Sa. H. mehr: . . . 1,25
Movement SA 14 day Strike "Silesia" full stock gears

① Spiral gong,
② Gloria gong, see TM-INDEX*
③ Domgong see page 33 and 99.
④ Harfen gong see TM-INDEX*, page 82.
⑤ Trio gong see TM-INDEX*, page 84.
⑥ 8 day solid plates movement 3/4 strike with Universalgong No.1

(*) Asterisk refers to the TRADEMARK-INDEX Antique Clocks Publishing, 1981 Edition.

Plate 45

Katalog-Seite	№	WEIGHT-CABLE-REGULATORS **Gewicht-Saitenzug-Regulateure** 7" = 18¼ cm oder 8" = 21 cm Email-Zifferblatt, Linsenpendel glatte, gelbe Gewichte	G. 8 Tag massives Gewichtszug-Schlagw., Tonfeder		Gg. 8 Tag massives Gewichtszug Gehwerk		8 day heavy d weight mover
			7" Blatt	8" Blatt	7" Blatt	8" B
83	1554	Nußbaum Walnut	86,—	87,50	74,75	76,2
82	1725	„	79,—	80,50	67,75	69,2
„	„	Eiche gebeizt Oak stained	88,—	89,50	76,75	78,2
83	1733	Nußbaum Walnut	85,—	86,50	73,75	75,2
82	1829	„	79,—	80,50	67,75	69,2
84	1900	„	—	83,—	—	76,75
„	„	Eiche gebeizt Oak stained	—	88,—	—	76,75
	G. u. Gg.	Movement without case **Das lose Werk ohne Gehäuse kostet:**	43,50	44,50	32,25	33,25

Weights without lead
Gewichte ohne Füllung weniger .... bei G: 2,50 bei Gg: 1,25
Eiche roh gegen Eiche gebeizt weniger Oak natural-not stained . 2,50
Elfenbein-Email- oder bedrucktes Silberzifferblatt erhöht bei 7": 1,— bei 8": 1,25
Ivory-enamel-or printed silverface
Universalgong Nr. 1 oder Stabgong Nr. 3 erhöht gegen Tonfeder 2,50
Universal gong No.1 or rod gong

8 day heavy dut
weight movem.
Strike Spiralgo

Katalog-Seite	№	MODERN WEIGHT-CABLE SALOON-REGULATORS **Moderne Gewicht-Saitenzug-Salon-Regulateure** 8" = 21 cm Silberzifferblatt, Linsenpendel, glatte, gelbe Gewichte	G. 8 Tag mass. Gewichtszug Schlagwerk Stabgong Nr. 3 oder Universalgong Nr. 1
86	1846	Nußbaum oder Eiche gebeizt. Walnut or oak stained	96,—
„	1846 L	Mahagoni poliert (einschl. Luxussteuer)	136,—
„	1847	Nußbaum. Walnut style stained	103,—
„	1847 L	Mahagoni poliert (einschl. Luxussteuer) Mahagoni polished	144,—
„	1868	Eiche gebeizt	96,—
„	1868 L	Mahagoni poliert (incl.luxery tax) Mahagoni poliert (einschl. Luxussteuer)	136,—
„	1869	Eiche gebeizt .. Oak stained	103,—
„	1869 L	Mahagoni poliert (einschl. Luxussteuer) Mahagoni polished (incl.luxery tax)	144,—
85	1871/55	Nußbaum oder Eiche gebeizt Walnut or oak stained	90,—
„	1877/55	Eiche gebeizt Oak stained	100,—
„	1878/55		107,—

The BOLD number refers to the page of this publication

Gewichte ohne Füllung weniger; Weights without lead . 2,50 bei L 2,75
Oak natural vs. Oak stained
Eiche roh gegen Eiche gebeizt weniger: 2,50
Gewichte u. Pendellinsen versilbert mehr: .... 0,75 bei L 0,85
Weight shell and pendulum disk silver plated.

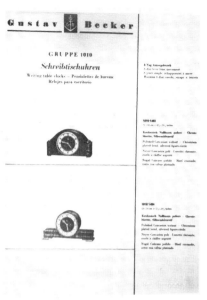

Plate 47
Catalogue No.22
Year 1933

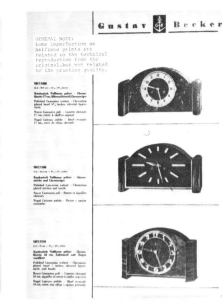

Plate 48
Catalogue No.22
1933

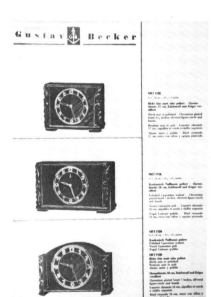

Plate 49
Catalogue No.22
1933

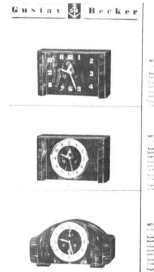

Plate 50
Catalogue No.22
1933

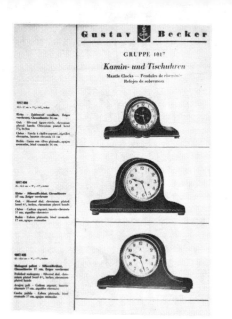

Plate 51
Catalogue No.22
1933

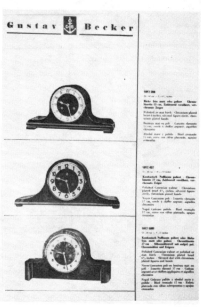

Plate 52
Catalogue No.22
1933

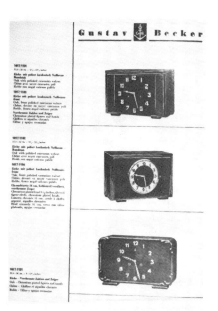

Plate 53
Catalogue No.22
1933

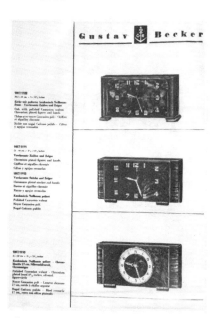

Plate 54
Catalogue No.22
1933

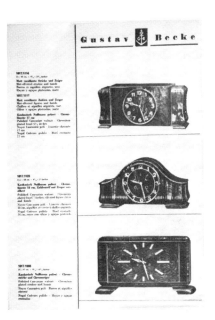

Plate 55
Catalogue No.22
1933

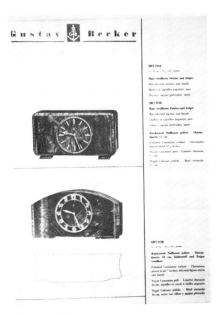

Plate 56
Catalogue No.22
1933

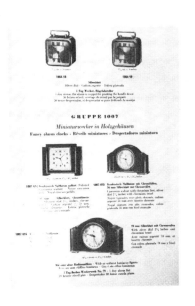

Plate 57
Catalogue No.22
1933

Plate 58
Catalogue No.22
1933

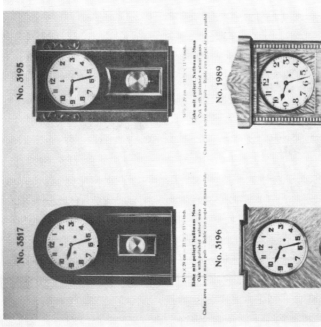

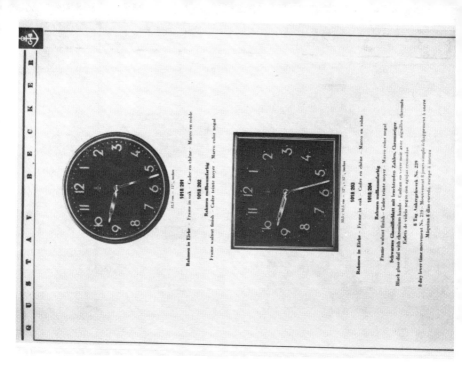

Plate 59a (L)
Catalogue No. 22
1933
Plate 59b (R)

BECKER SYNCHRON

Oak with walnut veneer,17 cm bezel-chapter ring,hands silver plated or 17 cm gold plated chapter ring, hands flat gold plated.

Fiche mit Kaukasisch Nußbaumfront
917 1209 a
17 cm Chromlünette, Zahlenreifen und Zeiger versilbert
917 1209 b
17 cm polierte Goldlünette, Zahlenreifen und Zeiger mattgold

Nußbaum fein matt
1017 1227
18 cm polierte Goldlünette, Zahlenreifen und Zeiger mattgold
Synchron-Gehwerk oder Synchron-Schlagwerk einfacher Gong oder Bim-Bam-Gong, 3 Stäbe
18 cm polished gold plated bezel, chapter ring and hands flat gold plated.
Single gong or BIM-BAM gong,3 rods.

BECKER SYNCHRON

Plate 60a (L)

Catalogue No.43
Year 1935

Plate 60b (R)

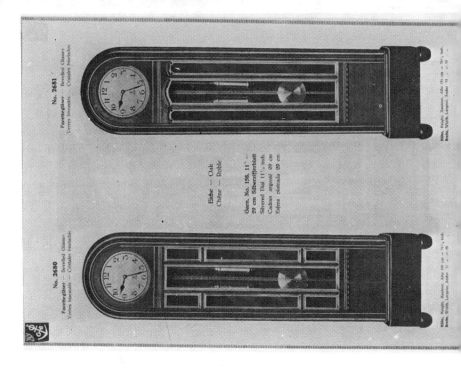
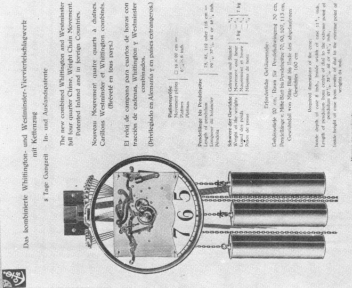

GUSTAV BECKER

GRUPPE 100S

Wecker mit Kleinwerk No. 250 Alarm clocks with smallest movement
Réveils avec le plus petit mouvement Despertadores con máquina pequeñita

1008 108 **Vernickelt** Nickelled Nickelé
Napolado

1008 131 **Vernickelt, gepreßte Messingwand.**
Nickelled, brass back
Nickelé, couvercle en laiton
Napolado, respaldo en latón

GENERAL NOTE:
Some imperfection on
halftone prints are
related to the technical
reproduction from the
original, but not related
to the printing quality.

Mit oder ohne Radiumziffern With or without luminous figures
Avec ou sans chiffres lumineux — Con ó sin cifras luminosas

GUSTAV BECKER

GRUPPE 100S

Wecker mit Kleinwerk No. 250 Alarm clocks with smallest movement
Réveils avec le plus petit mouvement Despertadores con máquina pequeñita

GRUPPE 100S

Wecker mit Kleinwerk No. 250 Alarm clocks with smallest movement
Réveils avec le plus petit mouvement Despertadores con máquina pequeñita

1008 100 **Vernickelt, gefaltetes Gehäuse**
Nickelled Nickelé Napolado

1008 101 **Rotbraun** Claret coloured
Brun-rouge Rojo oscuro

1008 102 **Blau** Blue Bleu Azul

1008 103 **Vernickelt** Nickelled Nickelé
Napolado

1008 105 **Rotbraun** Claret coloured
Brun-rouge Rojo oscuro

1008 106 **Blau** Blue Bleu Azul

1008 107 **Grün** Green Vert Verde

1008 104 **Vernickelt, staubdicher Reguliersehlitz.** Nickelled, dustproof regulating slot. Nickelé, fente de réglage hermétique. Napolado, hendidura de ajuste hermética.

Mit oder ohne Radiumziffern With or without luminous figures
Avec ou sans chiffres lumineux — Con ó sin cifras luminosas

15.9.35

Plate 62a (L)
Catalogue No. 35
1935
Plate 62b (R)

GUSTAV BECKER

GRUPPE 1008

Wecker mit Kleinstwerk No. 250 — Alarm clocks with smallest movement
Réveils avec le plus petit mouvement — Despertadores con máquina pequeñita

1008 114 Blau — Blue — Bleu — Azul
1008 115 Grün — Green — Vert — Verde
1008 116 Rotbraun — Claret coloured — Brun-rouge — Rojo oscuro
1008 138 Vernickelt — Nickelled — Nickelé — Niquelado

1008 117 Rotbraun — Claret coloured — Brun-rouge — Rojo oscuro
1008 120 Grün — Green — Vert — Verde
1008 118 Vernickelt — Nickelled — Nickelé — Niquelado
1008 119 Blau — Blue — Bleu — Azul

Mit oder ohne Radiumziffern — With or without luminous figures
Avec ou sans chiffres lumineux — Con ó sin cifras luminosas

GUSTAV BECKER

GRUPPE 1008

Wecker mit Kleinstwerk No. 250 — Alarm clocks with smallest movement
Réveils avec le plus petit mouvement — Despertadores con máquina pequeñita

1008 135 Rotbraun — Claret coloured — Brun-rouge — Rojo oscuro
Weißes Kartonblatt — White cardboard dial — Cadran carton blanc — Esfera blanca de cartón

1008 136 Verchromt mit blauem Band — Chromium plated with blue centre-band — Chromé avec bande bleue — Cromado con cinta azul
Metallblatt — Metal dial — Cadran métal — Esfera de metal

1008 137 Verchromt, mit elfenbeinfarbigem Band, bombiertem Glas — Chromium plated with centre-band, varnished ivory dull, convex glass — Chromé avec bande peinture ivoire laquée dépolie, verre bombé — Cromado con cinta barniz pálido mate, marfil, cristal biselado
Metallblatt mit verchromten Zahlen, Radium-Punkte und -Zeiger — Metal dial with chromium plated figures, luminous points and hands — Cadran métal avec chiffres chromés, points et aiguilles chromés — Esfera de metal con cifras cromadas, puntos y agujas luminosas

GRUPPE 1010

1010 1495 Mit aufgelegten Chromzahlen und -zeigern, ohne Lünette
Chromium plated figures and hands, without bezel
Chiffres et aiguilles chromés, sans lunette
Cifras y agujas cromadas, sin biselado

1010 1496 Mit 160 mm Chromlünette und bedrucktem Silberzahlenreif
With chromium plated bezel 6¼ inches, silvered figure-circle and hands
Avec lunette chromée 160 mm, aiguilles et cercle à chiffres argentés
Bisel cromado 160 mm, cifras y agujas plateadas

1010 1497 Kaukasisch Nußbaum – Caucasian walnut – Noyer caucasien – Nogal cáucaso
Birke poliert – Birch polished – Bouleau poli
Abedul pulido

1010 1498 Aufgelegte Chromzahlen und Chromzeiger, ohne Lünette
Chromium plated figures and hands, without bezel
Chiffres et aiguilles chromés, sans lunette
Cifras y agujas cromadas, sin bisel

1010 1499 Kaukasisch Nußbaum – Caucasian walnut – Noyer caucasien – Nogal cáucaso
Birke poliert – Birch polished – Bouleau poli
Abedul pulido

1010 1500 14,5 cm Chromlünette, bedruckter Silberzahlenreif und Silberzeiger
Chromium plated bezel 5¾ inches, silvered figure-circle and hands
Lunette chromée 14,5 cm, aiguilles et cercle à chiffres argentés
Bisel cromado 14,5 cm, cercos con cifras y agujas plateadas

8 Tag Ankerwerk No. 239 – 8 day lever time movement No. 239
Mouvement 8 jours simple à ancre No. 239
Maquina 8 dias cuerda, escape à áncora No. 239

1018 5 Nußbaum antik fein matt, polierte Goldlünette 18 cm, matt vergoldete Reef mit aufgelegten polierten Goldzahlen und Goldzeigern
Antique walnut mat, polished gilt bezel 7 inches, gilt hands, mat gilt circle with polished gilt raised figures
Noyer antique mat, lunette dorée polie 18 cm, aiguilles dorées, cercle doré mat avec chiffres appliqués dorés polis
Nogal antique mate, bisel dorado pulido 18 cm, agujas doradas, cerco dorado mate, con cifras doradas pulidas y sobrepuestas

8 Tag Ankerwerk No. 239
8 day lever time movement No. 239 Mouvement 8 jours simple à ancre
Maquina 8 dias cuerda, escape à áncora

1018 6 8 Tag Ankerwerk No. 239 – 8 day lever time movement No. 239
Mouvement 8 jours simple à ancre No. 239 – Maquina 8 dias cuerda à áncora No. 239

1018 7 14 Tag Schlagwerk "Bim Bam" 3 Stäbe
14 day pendulum strike movement "Bim Bam" gong 3 rods
15 jours sonnerie gong "Bim Bam" 3 tiges
14 dias sonería gong "Bim Bam" 3 varillas

Nußbaum antik braunsatt, Lünette, Zahlen und Zeiger matt vergoldet
Antique walnut fine mat, mat-gilt bezel, figures and hands
Nogal antique-lino mate, bisel, cifras y agujas doradas mate
Lunette Royal – Lunette – Bisel 17 cm = 6¾ inches

Plate 64a (L)

Catalogue No. 35 1935

Plate 64b (R)

GRUPPE 1024
Moderne Wanduhren, extra flach
Art Regulators, extra plat · Régulateurs modernes, extra plat
Reguladores de estilo moderno, extra planos

1024 301 Glattes Glas / Plain glass / Verre plat / Vidrio ordinario
1024 302 Facettglaser / Bevelled glasses / Verres biseautés / Cristales biselados

Silberblatt / Silver dial / Cadran argenté / Esfera plateada

7″ = 18,5 cm = 7¼ inches

1024 303 Glattes Glas / Plain glass / Verre plat / Vidrio ordinario
1024 304 Facettglaser / Bevelled glasses / Verres biseautés / Cristales biselados

Silberblatt / Silver dial / Cadran argenté / Esfera plateada

8″ = 21 cm = 8¼ inches

52 · 29 cm = 20½ × 11½ inches

Eiche mit Nußbaum · Oak with walnut · Chêne avec noyer · Roble con nogal

1024 304 26 / 1024 302 26

62 · 29 cm = 20½ × 11½ inches

Eiche mit Nußbaum, mit Messing- oder Ornamentbogen
Oak with walnut, plat, chromium bevelled glasses
Chêne avec noyer, plat, vitrages chromés
Roble con nogal, plano, cristales cromados

1024 302 28 Silberblatt / With silver dial 7½ inches / Cadran argenté 7″ / Esfera plateada 7″

1024 304 26, 28 and 29 mit 8″ Silberblatt
With silver dial 8¼ inches
Cadran argenté 8″
Esfera plateada 8″

Bim Bam-Gong No. 30/9-2 Schlag
Gong "Bim Bam" No. 30/9, 3 rods. – 3 tiges - 3 varillas

GRUPPE 1027
Wanduhren, normale Tiefe
Regulators, normal depth · Régulateurs, profondeur normale
Relojes de pared, profundidad normal

64 · 29 cm = 24 · 11½ inches

1027/3196
Eiche mit Kaukasisch Nußbaum
Oak with Caucasian walnut
Chêne avec noyer caucasien
Roble con nogal caucasiano

8″ = 21 cm Silberzifferblatt
8¼ inches silvered dial
Cadran argenté 8″ = 21 cm
Esfera plateada 8″ = 21 cm

68 · 29 cm = 27¼ × 11½ inches

1027/3196
Eiche mit poliert Nußbaum-Masa
Oak with polished walnut Masa
Chêne avec noyer poli Masa
Roble con nogal pulido Masa

Aufzug 3/9, Dampfanzugzug 1/9 (Bim Bam) 6/4 Westminsterschlag
Going "Bim Bam" / Svea or Dampgshlate, 6/4 Westminster chime
Going "Bim Bam" / Svea ou Dampgshlate, 6/4 Westminster
Going "Bim Bam" / Svea ó Dampgshlate, 6/4 Carillon Westminster

Plate 66a (L)

Catalogue No.35 1935

Plate 66b (R)

GRUPPE 1026

Wanduhren, extra flach

Art Regulators, extra plat - Régulateurs modernes, extra plat - Reguladores de estilo moderno, extra planos

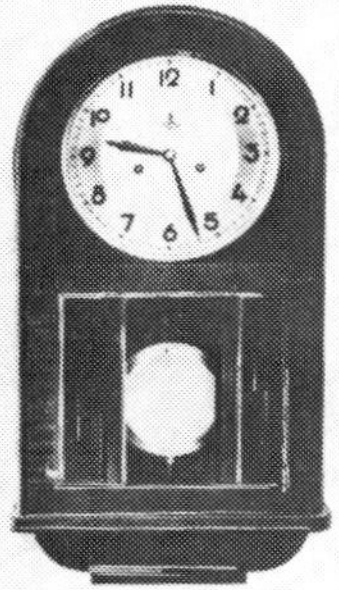

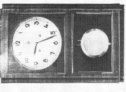

1026 3523 Glattes Glas – Plain glass
Verre plat – Vidrio ordinario

1026 3524 Facettegläser – Bevelled glasses – Verres biseautés – Cristales biselados

7" = 18,5 cm Silberblatt
Silver dial 7¼ inches
Cadran argenté 7" = 18,5 cm
Esfera plateada 7" = 18,5 cm

1026 3525 Glattes Glas – Plain glass
Verre plat – Vidrio ordinario

1026 3526 Facettegläser – Bevelled glasses – Verres biseautés – Cristales biselados

8" = 21 cm Silberblatt
Silver dial 8¼ inches
Cadran argenté 8" = 21 cm
Esfera plateada 8" = 21 cm

56 × 30,5 cm = 22 × 12 inches

Eiche mit Nußbaum – Oak with walnut, plat – Chêne avec noyer, plat – Roble con nogal, plano

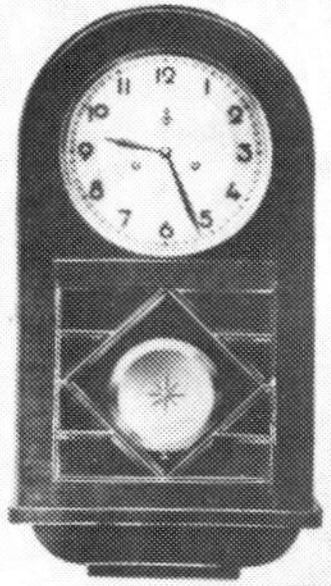

56 × 30,5 cm = 22 × 12 inches

1026 3524 27 **1026 3526 27**

1026 3524 26, 27, 30 mit 7" Silberblatt
With silver dial 7¼ inches
Avec cadran argenté 7"
Con esfera plateada 7"

Eiche mit Nußbaum, mit Messing- oder Chromverglasungen – Oak with walnut, plat, chromium bevelled glasses – Chêne avec noyer, plat, vitrages chromés – Roble con nogal, plano, cristales cromados

1026 3524 30 **1026/3526/30**

1026/3526 26, 27, 30 mit 8" Silberblatt
With silver dial 8¼ inches
Avec cadran argenté 8"
Con esfera plateada 8"

„Bim Bam" Gong No. 30/9: 3 Stäbe – Gong „Bim Bam" No. 30/9: 3 rods – 3 tiges – 3 varillas

GRUPPE 1027

Wanduhren, extra flach

Art Regulators, extra plat - Régulateurs modernes, extra plat - Reguladores de estilo moderno, extra planos

54 × 30 cm = 21¼ × 12 inches

1027 108

51 × 30 cm = 20¼ × 12 inches

1027 109

Kaukasisch Nußbaumfront poliert, Hinterkasten Eiche
Oak with Caucasian walnut, silver dial 8¼ inches with silvered pendulum-bob
Chêne avec noyer caucasien, cadran et lentille argenté
Roble con nogal caúcaso, esfera y lenteja plateada

54 × 30 cm = 21¼ × 12 inches

1027 111

Eiche – Oak – Chêne – Roble

54 × 30 cm = 21¼ × 12 inches

1027 107

Eiche mit kaukasisch Nußbaumfront
Oak with Caucasian walnut, silver dial 8¼ inches with silvered pendulum-bob
Chêne avec noyer caucasien, cadran et lentille argenté
Roble con nogal caúcaso, esfera y lenteja plateada

Zifferblatt – Dial – Cadran – Esfera 8" = 21 cm

Facettegläser – Bevelled glasses – Verres biseautés – Cristales biselados

„Bim Bam" Gong No. 30/9: 3 Stäbe – Gong „Bim Bam" No. 30/9: 3 rods – 3 tiges – 3 varillas

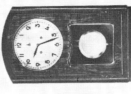

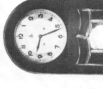

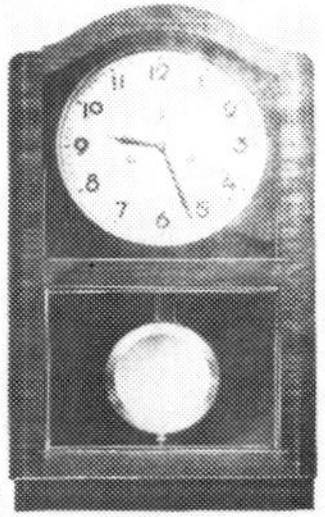

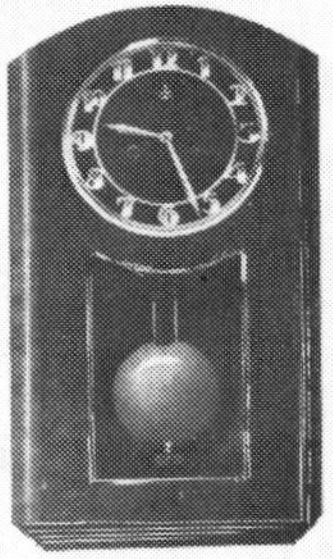

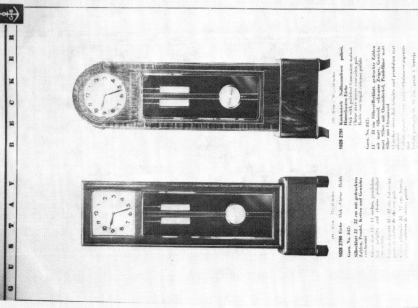

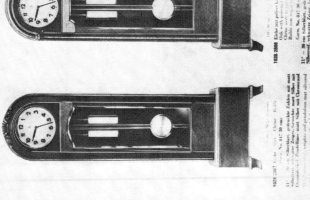

GRUPPE 17

Kleine Kamin- und Tischuhren mit ¼ „Bijou"-Westminsterschlag

Small mantle clocks with full ¼ Westminster chime movement „Bijou"
Petites pendules de cheminée avec carillon Westminster „Bijou"
Relojes pequeños de sobremesa con carillón Westminster „Bijou"

Bijou

8 Tag massiv ¼ Rechenschlagwerk auf Westminstergong
Einfachste Behandlung
Herausnehmbare Federhäuser

8 day solid ¼ rack strike movement
Westminster chime
Easy handling
Detachable barrels

□ 86 × 89 mm = 3⅜ × 4½ inch.

Mouvement massif 8 jours à râteau
¼ carillon Westminster
Manipulation très simple
Barillets démontables

Máquina maciza 8 días de sierra
¼ carillón Westminster
Simple manejo
Barriletes removibles

Cromwellian clock

1025 Messinggehäuse poliert
Polished brass case

8 Tag ¼ Westminsterschlag auf 5 Glocken
Pendel- oder 8. Ankergang

8 day full ¼ Westminster chime on 5 bells, solid pendulum movement or lever escapement best quality

23½ × 13 cm = 9¼ × 5⅛ inch.

Cromwellian clock

1025 Boite en cuivre poli
Caja en latón pulido

8 jours ¼ Carillon Westminster sur 5 timbres, mouvement massif à balancier ou à échappement à ancre soigné

8 días ¼ Carillón Westminster en 5 campanas máquina maciza con péndulo ó escape áncora fina

Silberzahlenreif 13½ cm — 5⁵⁄₁₆ inch. silvered mounted circle
Cercle argenté 13½ cm — Cerco plateado 13½ cm

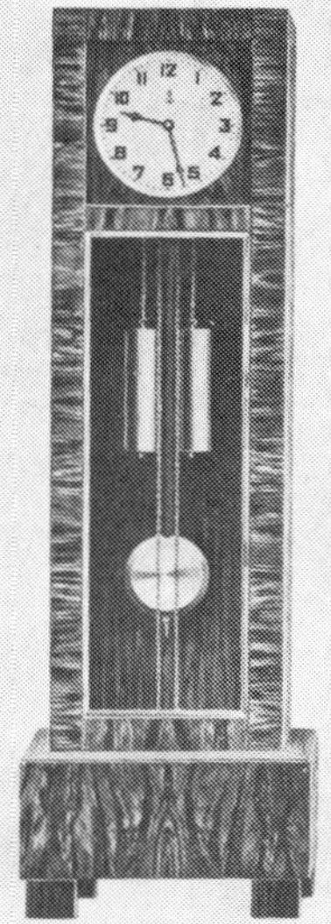

190 × 58 cm = 75 × 22¾ inch.

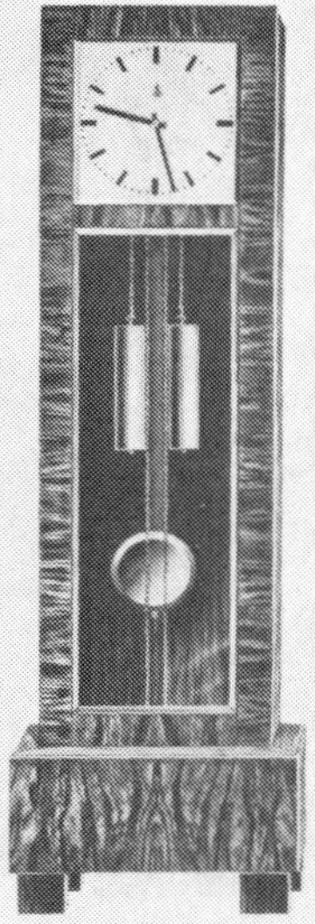

190 × 58 cm = 75 × 22¾ inch

2901 **2902**

Gabun mit pol. Kaukasisch Nußbaum-Front
Gaboon with caucasian (real) polished walnut
Gaboon avec noyer du caucase poli devant — Gaboon con nogal caucasiano pulido

Garn. No. 662:
Mattg. Zifferblatt 11" = 30 cm — 11⅞ inch. gilt dial
Cadran doré 11" = 30 cm — Esfera dorada 11" = 30 cm

Garn. No. 844:
Silberblatt 32 × 32 cm
Pendel, Gewichte und Ketten verchromt poliert
13 × 13 inch. silvered dial, pol. chrome pendulum, weights and chains polished
Cadran argenté 32 × 32 cm balancier, poids et chaines de chrome poli
Esfera plateada 32 × 32 cm lenteja, pesos y cadenas, de chromo pulido

Plate 68a (L)

Catalogue No. 20 Year 1931

Plate 68b (R)

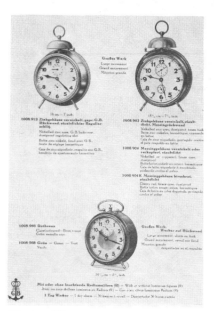

Plate 69
Catalogue No.20
Year 1931

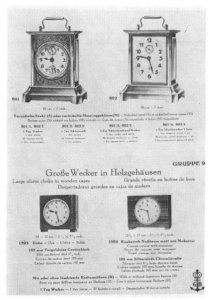

Plate 70
Catalogue No.20
1931

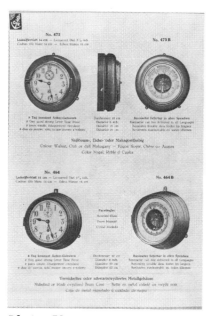

Plate 71
Catalogue No.20
1931

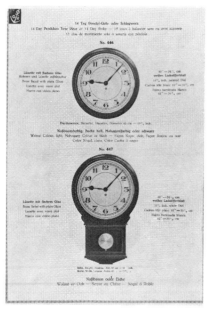

Plate 72
Catalogue No.20
1931

Plate 73
Catalogue No.44
Year 1935

Plate 74
Catalogue No.44
1935

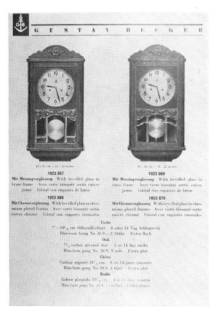

Plate 75
Catalogue No.44
1935

Plate 76
Catalogue No.44
1935

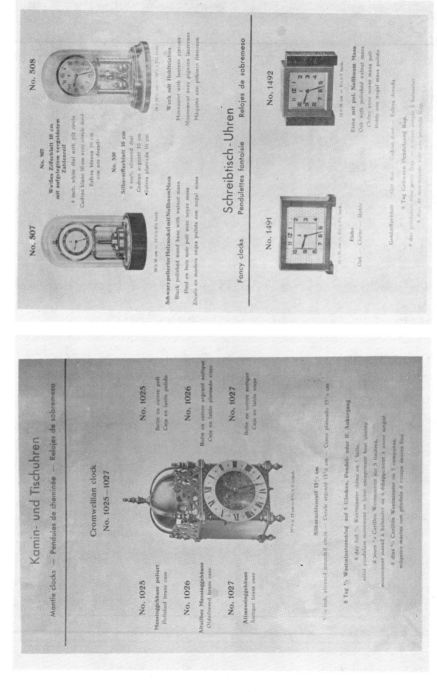

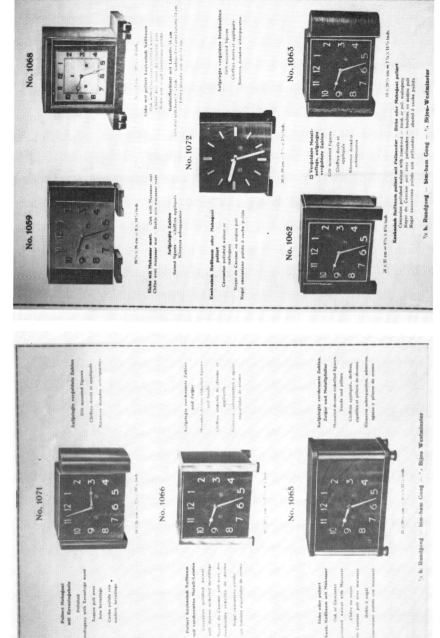

The Advantages

of the patent 14 day ½ hour "BIM-BAM" Strike Movement with Dom Gong No. 5/9 (5 rods).

1. This movement will go and strike with 5 hammers full 16 days.
2. The hammer pieces have been placed low down and are fixed outside the movement plates at the bottom part of the movement and so can be removed if necessary arises without taking the movement to pieces. The action of lifting the hammers is brought about by a very ingenious lifting work which requires very little power. This allows much longer and braver hammers with heavy hammer heads to be used, which, owing to their radius will fall by there own gravity on to the gong rails, these having faces tuned to a clear musical pitch, so that a remarkable volume of sound is obtained which surpasses anything hitherto been possible in regulators.
3. The **barrels are detachable** and are protected with holes for oiling the springs. After unscrewing the 2 small bridges on the front plate the barrels can be removed without taking the movement to pieces.
4. The movement so fitted with the "noiseless" Becker Rack which has proved a great success during the last 20 or more years.

Advantages

du mouvement déposé 15 jours sonnerie Bim-Bam ½ h, avec sonnerie Domgong n° 5/9 (5 tiges).

1. Le mouvement marche et sonne avec 5 marteaux, 16 jours pleins.
2. Les arbres de marteaux sont très bas et placés à l'extérieur de la platine et facilement interchangeables sans démontage du mouvement. Ils sont actionnés par un très ingénieux déclenchement de force. A cause de cela on peut employer des marteaux plus longs et plus lourds pouvant être employés et qui, par leur angle d'inclinaison, tombent avec leur propre poids et avec une grande force sur les gongs très nettement et harmonieusement accordés, de sorte que l'on a **une harmonie merveilleuse** jamais encore obtenue dans des horloges murales.
3. Les **barillets démontables** sont munis de trous pour l'huile; en dévissant les 2 petits ponts qui se trouvent sur la platine avant, on peut enlever les barillets sans démonter le mouvement.
4. Le mouvement a la construction de râteau "Becker" qui se fait depuis de nombreuses années, qui a toujours donné satisfaction et qui tourne sans bruit.

Ventajas

del sistema patentado de las máquinas 15 d.c. con sonería Bim-Bam ½ h. Domgong No. 5/9 (5 varillas).

1. Esta máquina marcha y toca la hora con cinco martillos durante 16 días completos.
2. Los ejes de los martillos son montados en un pequeño de la parte baja de la máquina, pero fuera de ella, siendo movidos éstos por una ingeniosa palanca construida para ahorrar fuerza, funcionan con un gasto mínimo de fuerza pudiéndose cambiar los ejes sin necesidad de desmontar las platinas. Este sistema permite el empleo de martillos con mayores largos, pesados y de mucha carrera, los que, debido a su gran ángulo de inclinación, caen con gran fuerza sobre los tubos gong del más limpio sonido musical, proporcionando a nuestros relojes de pared una sonoridad maravillosa.
3. Los **barrilletes son desmontables** y tienen agujeros engrasadores. Quitando los dos puentes pequeños de la platina delantera pueden sacarse los cubos sin necesidad de desmontar la máquina.

Neuheit!
Nouveauté!
Novedad!

Werke für moderne Wand- und Salonuhren
Movements for wall clocks of modern styles
Mouvements pour régulateurs modernes
Máquinas para reguladores modernos

Sa. HR. Gong No. 5/9 Bim-Bam
Sa. R. Gong No. 5/9 Bim-Bam

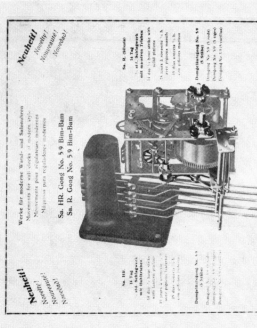

Sa. HR.
14 Tag
std. Schlagwerk
mit Stabbrettchen

14 day ½ hour strike with rod chimes

15 jours à sonnerie ½ h. avec gong à baguettes

15 días sonería ½ h. con gong con varillas

Sa. R. (Stista)
14 Tag
std. Schlagwerk
mit massiven Triebsen

14 day ½ hour strike with massive pinions

15 jours à sonnerie ½ h. avec pignons massifs

15 días sonería ½ h. con piñones macizos

Domgeläutegang No. 5/9
(5 Stäbe)

Domgong No. 5/9 (rods)
Domgong No. 5/9 (5 tiges)
Domgong No. 5/9 (5 varillas)

Vorzüge

des patentamtlich geschützten

14 Tag ½ **std. Bim-Bam Schlagwerkes mit Domgeläutegang No. 5/9 (5 Stäbe)**

1. Das Werk geht und schlägt mit 5 Hämmern volle 16 Tage.
2. Die Hammerwellen sind tief unten und außerhalb des Werkgestells an der unteren Platinenkante gelagert und ohne Zerlegen des Werkes auswechselbar. Sie werden durch ein sinnreiches, kraftsparendes Hebewerk bewegt, dadurch können längere und schwerere Hämmer mit stattlichen Hammerköpfen verwendet werden können, die infolge ihres Neigungswinkels mit größer eigener Schwere auf die musikalisch rein abgestimmten Gongstäbe fallen, so daß die bei Wanduhren bisher unbekannte wundervolle Tonfülle erzielt wird.
3. Die **herausnehmbaren Federhäuser** sind mit Öllöchern versehen. Durch Abschrauben der beiden kleinen auf der Vorderplatine befindlichen Brücken kann man die Federhäuser ohne Zerlegen des Werkes herausnehmen.
4. Das Werk hat die seit Jahrzehnten bewährte, nie versagende, gerauschlose Beckersche Rechenkonstruktion.

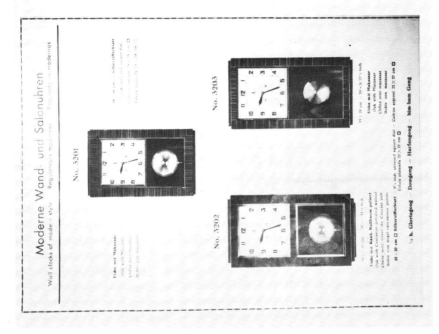
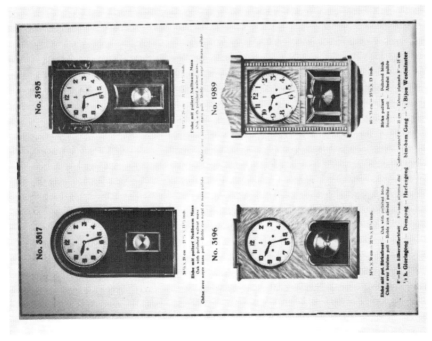

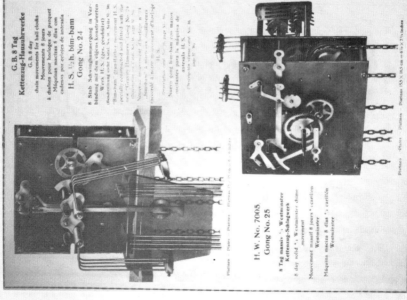

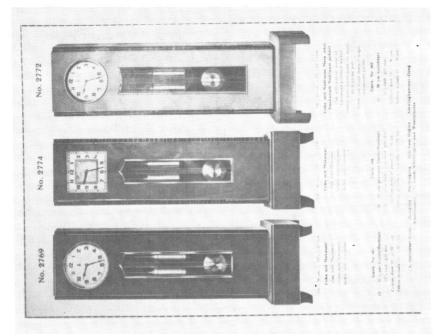
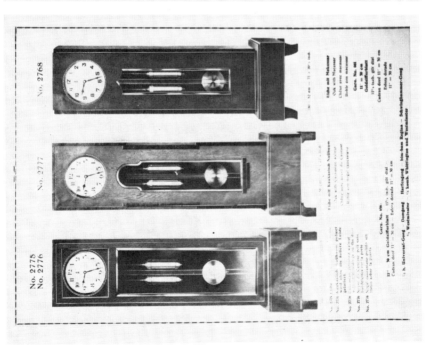

Plate 82a (L)
Catalogue No.17
Plate 82b (R)

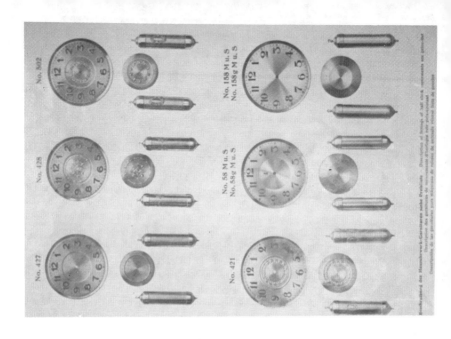

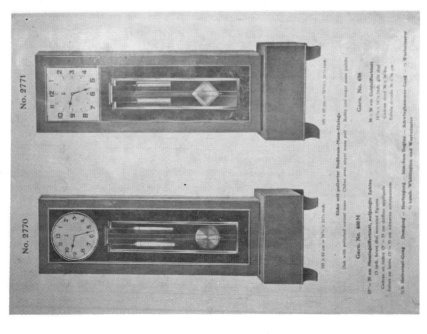

CHAPTER VII
PHOTOGRAPHIC PLATES and ARCHIVE DATA.

The photographic plates on the following pages,90-107 show a variety of GUSTAV BECKER clocks from private clock collectors and catalogues.The Gustav Becker clockmaking enterprise produced an abundance of clocks. The plates in this publication interduce to the reader typical GUSTAV BECKER clocks,the Gustav Becker enterprise also pruduced clocks , made to order.

Limited space in this publication did not permit an detail description of each timepiece, but historically exeptional clocks are emphasized. Co-Author Joh.Hennig compares a typical Becker alarm clock design with the famous French-made alarm clocks.
Included are detailed photographs of various movements such as the very rare "Schablonen-Uhr" (Pattern clock) Other clock movements show the influence of the Vienna Clockmaking tradition; after all, Gustav Becker begun his trade in Vienna - Austria.

Over the past several years, many readers sent photographs, description, and technical details of their Becker clocks. Unfortunately, the photographs were not of printing-camera reproduction quality, regretfully it was not possible to publish them.Proper credit for all photographic material is given on page 113.

ARCHIVE DATA,

The 1992 GUSTAV BECKER STORY contains additional data. In 1985, Herr Peter Starsy, horological researcher , of Neubrandenburg (formerly East Germany) published in " SCHMUCK & UHREN " (Jewellery and Clocks/watches) "GUSTAV BECKER BECKER 1819 - 1885, die Geschichte einer Uhrenfabrik " (the story of the Gustav Becker Clock enterprise) Herr Starsy had access to documents in the former East Germany archives. 1987 Herr Starsy published in "FREUNDE ALTER UHREN" (Friends cf old clocks) the "BISMARK UHR ".

In addition Herr Reinhard Schmitz, Germany, published in "ALTE UHREN" - Callwey Publishing Munich,year 1990 a detail essay describing the "BISMARK UHR" several very good illustrations underscore the outstanding top craftsmanship of the "BISMARK CLOCK".

Additional data,see page 109, BECKER family year 1782-1885

All these findings contribute to the history of the former GUSTAV BECKER enterprise. Proper credit is given on page 112. ■

Plate 84a
Very early model travel alarm clock, made by *MAUREL-PARIS, France*, year unknown (1850-1860?)

Plate 85b
Back of the *MAUREL* travel alarm clock, one of the first models widely marketed.

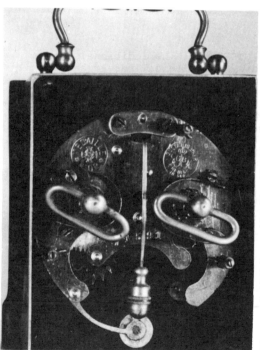

Also see page 97
for reference

French inspired GUSTAV BECKER travel alarm clock with improved design features. Marketed to gain independence from French imports.
Spring: Encased
Escapement: Roll type, not sensitive for slight variation of the level base.
Gears: Full stock
Face: Enameled
Alarm: Front setting.

Plate 85

Plate 86
GUSTAV BECKER alarm mantle clock

Plate 87
Backplate, windup and setting, note the stub type pendulum.

Plate 88
GUSTAV BECKER alarm mantle clock, walnut veneer case, gold gilded decor.

Plate 89
View of the back opening (cover plate removed)

Plate 90
Light oak case, petite wall
clock. Bevelled glass, half-
full hr strike, spiral gong.

Plate 91
Movement back plate, clock
made @ 1920, GUSTAV BECKER
WORKS Braunau-Czechoslovakia.

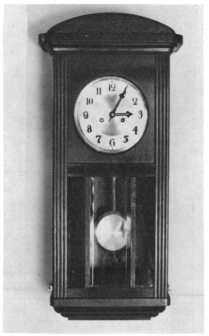

Plate 92
GUSTAV BECKER wall clock,
half and full hr BIM-BAM
strike vintage @ year 1927.

Plate 93
Backplate (refer to page 32
for more details)

Plate 94
3 weight *GRAND SONIERE*, made by GUSTAV BECKER WORKS, repeat 1/4 hr strike, spiral gong.

Plate 95
GUSTAV BECKER *GRAND SONIERE*, repeater, etched face, weights & pendulum. Walnut case. @ 1895.

Plate 96
GUSTAV BECKER, 2 weight Vienese style regulator, half-full hr. strike. Made in Braunau.

Plate 97
View of the movement backplate note the slotted (patented movement support)

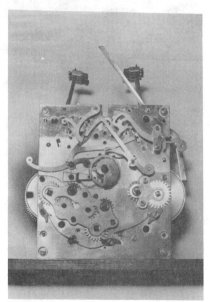

Plate 98
BECKER, Westminster mantle clock, patented spring barrel, silent rack fall. Year 2 1920

Plate 99
Backplate, note removable pivot plate for 1/4 hr chime drum. Model 444 world wide marketed

Plate 100
3 Weight GUSTAV BECKER movement. Year @ 1891, note the "Viennese" influenced design.

Plate 101
Backplate of movement plate 10 serial No. 800898, note the fin engraving on the weight pulley

Plate 102
GUSTAV BECKER, *BAROQUE GRAND SONIERE*, 3 weight repeater, full stock walnut case.

Plate 103
GUSTAV BECKER "*CARTEL*" clock, half-full hr. strike, spiral gong, gold leafed wood case.

Plate 104
GUSTAV BECKER, english style Westminster strike mantle clock. Fine walnut veneer case.

Plate 105
GUSTAV BECKER, 400 day disk Anniversary clock. (refer also to page   of this publication.

Plate 106
GUSTAV BECKER -*FREISCHWINGER*-
(freeswinger),@ 1898,half and
full hr.strike,spiral gong.

Plate 107
Open case view,an GUSTAV B]
design,allowing easy acces:
the movement.Pine-walnut v(
case.

Plate 108
Full brass decor pendulum,
casted in lost wax casting.

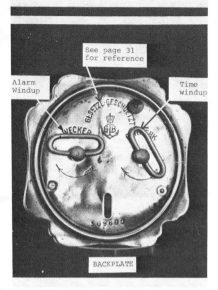

Plate 109a
Prototye of the mass produced
GUSTAV BECKER alarm clock,
production ended in the 1923.

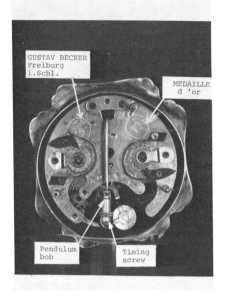

Plate 109b
Backplate removed of alarm clock.
Serial No. 509 600.

Plate 110
Pendulum-Alarm clock, made in France. Note the octacone style.

Plate 111
The GUSTAV BECKER version of the alarm clock shown on plate 111, front alarm setting lever, note the rounded corners.

Plate 113
Backplate view of the movement. Note the BECKER patent slotted movement support holes. Serial No. 2046??.

Plate 112
3 Weight *GRAND SONIERE* by GUSTAV BECKER Works, repeater strike, all engraved, walnut case.

Plate 114a
BECKER novelty clock, dog wiggles the tail.

Plate 114
2 Weight GUSTAV BECKER wall clock, half-full hr strike. Hardwood case ebony stained.

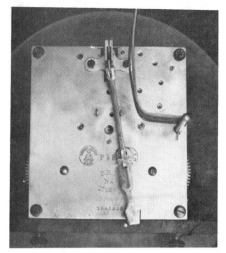

Plate 115
Backplate of movement, serial No. 1,945,399, especially made for the British marked.

Plate 116
Detail of the Rod gong, an all BECKER patented design. Note: D.R.P. (see also page 31)

Plate 116a
2 Weigth GUSTAV BECKER hall clock half-full hr. strike rod gong. Case full stock pine, walnut veneer solid walnut wood decor carving. Overall height 62", overall width 20 ½".

Private collector.

GUSTAV BECKER decor mantle clock.
Oak case
with all brass
embossed decor. The
godess figurines,
bronze lost wax
casting.
Half and full hr.
strike, spiral gong.
Thermometer on the
right side and
barometer on the
left in perfect
working order.
Serial No. 787289
(Year 1885-1890)
Height: 27" (661mm)
Width : 29" (710mm)
Figures:11" (270mm)
Projection
across front:14"
                (343mm)

Plate 117

Plate 118b

Plate 118a
The Frey family,Mr.Frey was a well to do merchant,owner of the "Norddeutschen Eis - werke" - Ice-Service.Family fell victim to the Inflation. Photograph year @ 1882

ooooooooo

This tall hall clock, all full stock oak,dark finish in very fine cabinet work. Door with bevelled glass. Solid machine finish clock works.Strikes every half & full hour, BIM-BAM. Patented silent rack fall, 8 day weight drop.Made by the GUSTAV BECKER, Freiburg clock factory year @ 1895. The clock bequeated from the Frey estate in Berlin to the great grandson and his family Mr.Frey,Martinez California.

Clock is now located at the Cultural Center "Schlesien-Haus" Königswinter, FRG, Germany

Plate 119
Decor nightstand pendulum alarm clock. Frame all bronze lost wax casting. Movement see also page 97. Vintage of this petite clock about end of the 19th century.

Plate 120
SCHABLONEN UHR*single model pattern clock
very unusual clock with the basic design
of the"VIENNESE SCHOOL"by GUSTAV BECKER.
* Pattern clock refer also to page 104 and lo5.

Plate 121
Front view of the *SCHABLONEN UHR**note the details of the repeater linkage,whiplash, detend arrestor,quarter rack hook,adjustment for the hammer fall.Year @ 1885.

Plate 122
The rear plate of the Pattern clock, shows the modification of the lower bridge, the suspension rod beat adjustment is a typical Gustav Becker patented feature. Additional helper spring.

Pattern clocks were experimental clocks, made for research, patent applications, and or marketing feasibility. In some case pattern clocks often ended up as dealers floor sample.

The backplate serial number, differs from the front plate serial number (page 104- plate 121) For the experiment, any material was used what ever was in stock.

Plate 123
Very rare matching pair of GUSTAV BECKER one weight regulator's. Case style influenced by the *VIENNESE* era.
The cases made of full stock pine wood, faced with walnut veneer. All decor full stock walnut. The clock on the left serial number 30,060 (@ year 1868), the clock on the right bears the serial number 4845 of the very early production (@ year 1861).

Plate 124
Gustav Becker, spring wound wall clock, half and full hr. strike. Spiral gong, immitation temperature compensation pendulum, R = Retarded (slow)
A = Advance (fast) indicator for the timing screw turning direction. Vintage @ 1900. The top decor at a later date replaced.

TRANSLATION DOCUMENT POSTMASTER GEN.GERMANY
From German into English

For the Main Contract.....the contractholder (G.Becker) must prove the payment of till.....of -ONE MARK / 50 PFENNIG.......

CONTRACTUAL AGREEMENT

...... the Clockmanufacturer G.B. in Freiburg/Silesia, behalf of manufacturing and delivery of Officeclocks for the Postal and Telegraph Administration under the 21/23 November, 1863 signed contract.
By order and in behalf of the German Empire General Postal Admistration, with the reservation of the expected permission, to day in connection with the German Empire Postoffice in Freiburg/Silesia and by.......von zur Westen (Postal director) and the Clockmanufacturer Gustav Becker the following addendum on Nov.? 21/23 at ....clock was signed.

Par.1

Mister G.Becker declares,his willingness, based on the contract vom....November 1863, the pending order (of office clocks) from now on to be reduced from the former price of....MARK(Goldmark) ....60 Pfennig.

Par.2

All other agreements in the contract from Nov.21/23, 1863 are valid and stay in power.

Par.3

The official fee for the Addendum-contractual-Agreement shall be paid by the manufacturer.
The present addendum is excuted in duplicate - same word text - and from both...... signed and witnessed and signed by two witnesses.

Freiburg Silesia 25.April 1871
signed by

STAMP   signed:von zur WESTEN   GUSTAV BECKER
         Postal Director
                                 SEAL   A.Friedrich Brueckner
                                          .....Inspector
Royal German Post office   signed by
FREIBURG   witness:
                                        ....

NOTE from the Publisher: ....dotted (ine in the sentence denotes ,that the word from the archive document is not legible.

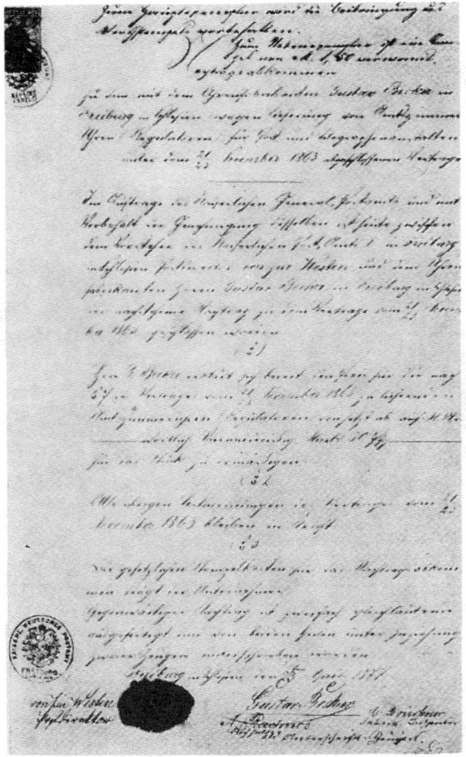

Plate 125
Addendum to the Contract - Agreement between the German Empire General Postmaster Berlin/Germany and Gustav Becker,Clockmaking Enterprise Freiburg

CHRONOLOGICAL DATA / 1782 - 1885
- BECKER -

Father of Gustav Becker	Johann Gottlieb Becker : * 1782 / + 1825 City Musician
Mother of Gustav Becker	: * 1791 / + 1858 Henriette Caroline Wilhelmine ne Schwarz.
Their son	:JOHANN GUSTAV EDUARD BECKER - GUSTAV BECKER -
Born, 2.May 1819	: Oels, Schlesien (now Olesnica - Poland)
Education	:Attended local schools, watchmaker apprentice Watchmaker journeyman in: Dresden, Germany Berlin, " Frankfurt - Main " Munich "
Visited, the hub of Swiss Watch/Clockmaking. Year unknown.	:La Chaux-de-Fonds, Switzerland,
1841	: Employment by Master Clockmaker Philipp Happacher of Vienna - Austria
1845 Watchmaker	: Opened his own Watchmaker Shop in Oels Silesia
1845 Married	: On October 2nd, Friedericke Henriette Louise Seelig * 1822 / + 1909 Fathered two sons and three daughters.
1847	: Announced opening of a clock making shop in Freiburg (see page 3)
1850	: Received his Business License.
1854	: Received exclusive contract to design and produce clocks for the offices of the German Postal administration
1875	: Titel of "Royal Commisioner" State of Prussia / Silesia.
1884	: Son Richard Becker and nephew Paul, became partner in the Becker Enterprise.
1885	: 14.September 18885 passed away in Berchtesgaden/Baver. Germany.

PLATE REFERENCE

Chapter I	Johannes Hennig	Page 1
	Stefan of Wroclaw Poland	Page 3,4,5,
Chapter II	Gerd Bender	Page 22,23,24,25,26, 27,28
Chapter III	Author	Page 29
	Johannes Hennig	Page 35,36
Chapter IV	Gerd Bender	Page 37,38
	Johannes Hennig	Page 39,40,41,42,43, 44,45,46,47,48, 49,50,51,52,53, 54,55,57,58,59, 60
Chapter V	Johannes Hennig	Page 61,62,63,64,65, 66
	Author	Page 67,68,69,70,71, 72,73,74,75,76, 77,78,79,80,81, 82
Chapter VI	Author	Page 92,93,96,99,101
	Johannes Hennig	Page 90,97,102
	Turner Gilman	Page 91,92
	Stan Good	Page 93,94
	N.L.Miller	Page 98 (Plate 114a)
	David H.Safier - Photo Grey	Page 98 (Plates 112 113)
	Clarence V.Hunt	Page 100
	Rudi Kemper - Photo Palmer -	Page 103,104.105.106 107

BIBLIOGRAPHY

* GUSTAV BECKER
    Obituary :DEUTSCHE UHRMACHERZEITUNG-(German Watch/Clockmaking Journal) 1885, Dec.1. Volume 9, page 141-143
* GUSTAV BECKER
    "DIE BISMARKUHR" (The Bismark Clock) DEUTSCHE UHRMACHER ZEITUNG.1885, Dec.1th, Vol.23 page 175.
* CARL SCHULTE
    "LEXIKON der UHRMACHERKUNST" (Dictionary of Watch/ Clockmaking Art)1902 (reprinted 1980,Leipzig form. East Germany),page 362.
* "DEUTSCHE UHRMACHER ZEITUNG" (German Watch/Clockmaking Journal) ,1881 - Oct.15. Vol.5,20, page 153-156. The clocks at the Trade Exhibition in Breslau-Silesia year 1881.
* WILHELM WOLFF
    "AUS SCHLESIEN-PREUSSEN & REICH"(Silesia-Prussia & German Empire),1985 Dietz-Publication Berlin.
* HAUPTSTAATSARCHIV STUTTGART/GERMANY
    "Vereinigte Freiburger Uhrenfabriken,vormals Gustav Becker, 1899 - 1924.Anniversary Publication.
* STARSY PETER
    "Schmuck und Uhren" 1985,Berlin Germany, "Schriften Freunde Alter Uhren" 1987 Vol.XXVI
* SCHMITZ,REINHARD
    "BISMARK UHR" - ALTE UHREN - Callwey Publication year 1990.

NOTE: * -astrik -PRINTED IN GERMAN LANGUAGE -

MESSAGE from the AUTHOR and PUBLISHER

Dear Reader,

About 23 years ago, my dear friend Johannes Hennig, of Hartha-Dresden-Germany, and I embarked on the horological research project of the GUSTAV BECKER STORY.

Few years later the modest Edition © 1974 was off the press.

During my research, travelling in many European countries, searching for information and data of the GUSTAV BECKER enterrise, I made many contacts.

My visits behind the "Iron curtain- East Germany" under the eyes of the ever present Staate Police-STASI- was risky and very stressful.

After my departure from East Germany, some of my contacts were later questioned.

To day, the "Nightmare East-Germany" is over, the wall is down.

The authors, Johannes Hennig and Karl Kochmann intended to travel to Gustav Becker's graveside in memory of the CENTENIAL death in the year 1885.

The toll of our advanced age, failing health and personal circumstances prevented both of us from making this pilgrimage.

Since the first Edition of the GUSTAV BECKER STORY, eight, improved, enlarged, reprinted Editions followed. The credit goes to many "Write in" owners of GUSTAV BECKER clocks with the desire to share theier clocks with others and to add photographs and data to the publisher archive.

I thank all my faithful readers, the horological booksellers in Austria, Germany, England, Switzerland. Special THANKS to AMERICAN REPRINTS Co. the General Agent of ANTIQUE CLOCKS PUBLISHING.

Sincerely, I hope, that all my efforts are of value to the clock collector, the historian, and all who just simply want to enhance theier knowledge of the subject "European Industrialized Clockmaking" ■

Concord, California
U.S.A.
August 1995

With best regards

Karl Kochmann
(Karl Kochmann)
Author
Private
Publisher

ACKNOWLEDGMENTS

Very special thanks to Herrn Johannes Hennig, Dreden-Hartha (now Germany), for providing and contributing much information for the GUSTAV BECKER STORY, it was the year 1973, when Herr Hennig under very difficult circumstances, living in the former "German Democratic Republic" (known as Communist East Germany) conduct correspondence and mailed photographs to the capitalistic West.

Herr Gerd Bender, horological author/researcher of Black Forest Clockmaking, especially for his generous gift to the author of the Gustav Becker Story, the anniversary printing : VEREINIGTE FREIBURGER UHREN-FABRIKEN, vormals GUSTAV BECKER ENTERPRISE, 1889-1924.

Mr. Bronislaw Shicker of California, for his search and visit to the Gustav Becker gravesite. Providing a recent photograph (1991) of the restored Becker marble relief.

Mr. T. Gilman, member of the National Association of Watch and Clock Collectors Inc.U.S.A. for photographs.

Mr. Rudi Kemper, Master Clockmaker, for rare photographs by Mr. Robert Palmer, member of the Cleveland Art Institute.

Herrn Peter Starsy of Neubrandenburg, Germany for his efforts to do further in depth research of the Gustav Becker - History.

The management of the Callwey Publishing Company, Munich - Germany, for the essay "BISMARK-UHR" in the Publication "UHREN" Vol.4, year 1990.■

THE BLACK FOREST
CLOCKMAKER
and the
CUCKOO CLOCK

11th Edition

240 Pages
5½ x 8½ "
perfect bound
plastic soft
cover.

. 38 CHAPTERS
. history,
. repairs,
. restoring of
  clock cases,
. patents,
. functional
  diagrams,
. table of clock
  age.
. Repair hints
  from Black
  Forest shop
  foreman's

TRADEMARK INDEX - 92
CLOCKS & WATCHES
of
European Origin

AUSTRIA   — ENGLAND
FRANCE   — GERMANY
SWITZERLAND

GENERAL   REVISED
EXPANDED   EDITION

5½ x 8½" 960 PAGES
perfect bound soft
plastic cover,

15,000 TRADEMARK
       WORDMARK
DATA.

ELECTRICAL CLOCKS

TABLES ORGANIZATION
of
Premier Watch/Clock
Manufacturer
+++++++++

FOR INFORMATION CONTACT THE BOOK DEPOSITORY'S
▶ ANTIQUE CLOCKS PUBLISHING SEE ◀
PAGE 114

ANTIQUE CLOCKS BOOK DEPOSITORY:

U.S.A.

WHOLESALE * CATALOG ON REQUEST * RETAIL
Worldwide Sales
of
Horological Books

$ SCANLON
American Reprints Co.

VISA   MASTERCARD
Doris & Loren Scanlon
P.O. Box 379, Modesto, CA 95353 U.S.A.
Phone (209) 667-2906   FAX (209) 521-2777
French/German Correspondence Welcome

S. LaRose, Inc.
Worldwide Distributors to Horologists

French/German/English Correspondence Welcome

Catalogue on Request   VISA/MASTERCARD accepted
3223 Yanceyville St., P.O. Box 21208, Greensboro, N.C. 27420, USA
Telephone: (919) 621-1936,   Fax Number: 1-800-537-4513

ENGLAND

RITA SHENTON LBHI
148 PERCY ROAD, TWICKENHAM,
TW2 6JG ENGLAND

INTERNATIONAL SALES – CATALOGUE ON REQUEST

BOOKS
New and Old

Telephone: 081 894 6884 (London) U.K.
FAX: 081 893 8766

AUSTRIA

UHRMACHERMEISTER
LUKAS STOLBERG

Horological Books - Uhrenliteratur - Catalogue on Request
A-8019 Graz, Grabenstrasse 9
Österreich - Austria
Telephon: 0316 - 30 26 53   FAX: 0316 - 30 26 53

French/German/English Correspondence Welcome

GERMANY

Wuppertaler Uhrenmuseum

JURGEN ABELER F.B.H.I
Uhren Goldschmuck Juwelen Edelsteine.
Uhren- und Schmuck-Fachliteratur
**Poststrasse 11
42 103 Wuppertal
Germany - FRG**
Tel: 0202/49300-0 FAX: 0202/49300-59
Credit Cards Welcome   KREDITKARTEN werden akzeptiert
English Correspondence Welcome

Advertisement courtesy of Antique Clocks Publishing

Plate 126
Birdeye view of the former
GUSTAV BECKER Enterprise,
first half of the XX Century.
Courtesy Clock Museum:
MUZEUM ZIBMI-Klodzko / Poland

PREFACE,

The 8th Edition of the GUSTAV BECKER STORY,contains on the following pages new archive material and photographs,historical data and updated information on the once worldwide famous GUSTAV BECKER enterprize.
On page 115,plate 127,a Premier class Hall Clock illustrates at best that the GUSTAV BECKER Enterprise catered to any costumers request in style and expense.
On page 116,plates 128-131,the *"JUGENDSTIL"*style*GUSTAV BECKER wall clock with the artistic brass works decor demostrates that the GUSTAV BECKER,Braunau-Bohemia works were engaged in very fine special costumer orders.Noteworthy is the embossement of the backplate serial number: 386447 and the stamping : BRAUNAU i.BOEHMEN,**
It is assumed,that the large number 3,followed by the five diget serial number indicates the production code of the GUSTAV BECKER-Braunau-Bohemia,plant,***

On page 119,plates 134-136,another testimony of the
GUSTAV BECKER enterprise to create and construct a exeptional rarely "Musical Clock".
Plate 126,is an airial view of the GUSTAV BECKER enterprise in Freiburg-Silesia,now Swibodzice-Poland.
It came to the authors attention,that in Klodzko-Poland the Cultural authorities manage a very fine public Clock Museum with many GUSTAV BECKER Clocks on display.■

NOTE:
    * *"JUGENDSTIL"* Architectual exterior/interior design style in central Europe between the years 1885 - 1914.
  ** see page 117,plate 132 (stamp -A-)
 *** see page 117,plate 133
  © Karl Kochmann 1995

Plate 127

GUSTAV BECKER, Hall clock, English "Portico" style top. Clock case, full stock walnut wood veneer clock case backplate "Herringbone" inlaid veneer.
Door and sides plain glass, secured with beechwood strips. Overall height 6'-6 1/2". Average front 1'- 11 1/2 ".

      Solid brass machined movement plates. Serial Number 111 94 30 , vintage @ year 1895. The silver plated brass stock dial with engraved Roman numbers filled with black letter seal wax. Seasoned wood pendulum stick with heavy 9 " diameter brass pendulum disk.

Private collector U.K.England. 000093

NOTE: Clock case and components in *"JUGENDSTIL"**design.
  *Design style in Europe between the years 1895-1914.

Plate 128
GUSTAV BECKER, 3 weight
"GRAND SONIERE"
Movement plate 386447
*Private Collector,
California U.S.A.*

Plate 129
Clock dial detail.

Plate 130
Clock weight detail.

Plate 131
Detail pendulumn disk

Plate 132
GUSTAV BECKER, 2 weight movement
back plate, serial Number 386447
A embossement: FREIB.i.SCHL.
  abbreviated FREIBURG in SCHLESIEN
B medaille d'or (Gold medal awarded)

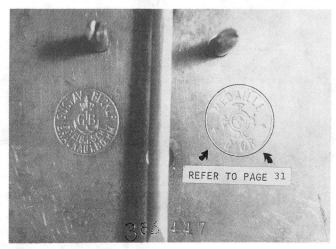

Plate 133
GUSTAV BECKER, 2 weight movement
back plate, serial Number 386447

Plate 135 Detail of the top, dial and wood decor.
The strike train lever connected with a rope to the the music box player release lever.

Plate 134.GUSTAV BECKER HALL Clock with metal disk playing music box.Full stock pine-hardwood laminated case, over all hight 76" (inch) 10 1/2 " wide, 12 1/2 " deep. Spring (2) powered movement, serial number: 1 196 808 (@ year 1896)

Private Collector, Birmingham, Alabama U.S.A.

Plate 136.Detail of the music box player section. Size of the metal disk 11 ",(inch) made in Leipzig - Germany. Selection of @ 30 tunes, like La paloma,Austrian military march,God save the Emperor (Austrian) Silent night etc.

Notes

Notes

Other Books From ClockWorks Press

BOOKS	Price	Quantity	Total
By Mr. Kochmann:			
Gustav Becker Story	$13.95		
Black Forest Clockmaker and the Cuckoo Clock 264 pgs. includes repair techniques	$25.95		
Clock and Watch Trademark Index 1000 pgs. hardcover	$38.50		
Black Forest Music Clocks 60 pgs. with color photos	$17.95		
Lenzkirch, Winterhalder & Hofmeier Clocks 138 pgs. with color photos	$13.95		
By Others:			
Clock Repair: Part-time Hours, Full-time Pay 200 pgs by John R. Pierson SB	$19.95		
Practical Clock Repairing 242 pgs. by Donald de Carle HB	$29.95		
The Modern Clock 512 pgs. by Ward Goodrich HB	$24.95		
Practical Clock Escapements 245 pgs. by Laurie Penman HB	$42.50		
Shipping: Free in USA. Overseas: Actual charges applied.			
Total:			

ClockWorks Press
P.O.Box 1699
Shingle Springs, California
U.S.A. 95682-1699
books@clockrepair.com
www.clockrepair.com
800-580-7701 or   530-677-7811
Contact us for free horological book catalog.